NEW CELTS

New Celts

New Celts

ROGER ELLIS AND CHRIS SEATON

KINGSWAY PUBLICATIONS
EASTBOURNE

Illustrations on pages ii, 110, 170 and 176 copyright © Pete Greig,
Outa This World Designs
Illustrations on pages 31 and 63 copyright © Ruth Cumming, Revelation
Church
Illustrations on page 79 copyright © Olivia Clarke, Revelation Church

Unless otherwise indicated, biblical quotations are
from the New International Version © 1973, 1978, 1984
by the International Bible Society.

Co-published in South Africa with SCB Publishers
Cornelis Struik House, 80 McKenzie Street
Cape Town 8001, South Africa
Reg no 04/02203/06

ISBN 0 85476 737 1

Designed and produced by Bookprint Creative Services
P.O. Box 827, BN21 3YJ, England for
KINGSWAY PUBLICATIONS
Lottbridge Drove, Eastbourne, E. Sussex, BN23 6NT.
Printed in Great Britain.

Contents

List of Illustrations

Foreword

We are the first post-modern generation. They describe us as having no sense of heritage or history and little hope for a better future. We are trapped in a perpetual present where all that counts is the here and now. This leads to shallow living without reflection or stability. 'If it feels good, do it' is the motto. This culture shift has influenced the church. Indeed one of the major criticisms of what used to be known as the charismatic movement (but is now too broad to have one clearly defined label) is that it is a touchy-feely superficial expression of Christianity, out of touch with both history and heritage.

This is a prophetic book. It is a book 'for such a time as this'. This is a book about the history of the British church, yet it is so much more than a history book. It is a prophetic book in that it unearths some amazing parallels between the state of the Celtic world and our own, between the mission of the Celtic church and the church as it approaches the third millennium. It is a passionate book as one would expect from Roger and Chris, but it is very much a book that enlightens the mind as well as warms the heart. We are challenged to rediscover a simple (yet not simplistic) faith for a complicated world. We are challenged to live a life of community and apparent powerlessness in political terms that we might be an expression of the love of heaven in the here and now.

I must confess I come to this subject of the Celts as a recent convert. I had been aware that many were making a study of the Celts, their worship, mission and lifestyle, and I inwardly groaned. 'Not another distraction,' I thought, 'from the ministry of the kingdom today.' I have repented. Through my own limited reading and discussions with Roger and Chris I have come to realise that we have many lessons to learn from our forefathers in the faith. The Celtic Christians knew how to be spontaneous and charismatic, relating to ordinary people. They were missionaries to their own culture. They were at one with creation and yet worshipped the Creator. They were prophetic to their culture in their lifestyles and yet were not aliens to it. We must learn these lessons for our times. These are days of such opportunity for the church of Jesus Christ.

As well as having a prophetic edge, this book is earthed in reality. It was not written in some ivory tower; the principles presented here are being worked out in Roger and Chris' own fellowship. Indeed this is what gives *New Celts* its credibility; there are not only references to fifth-century Northumbria but also to 1998 Sussex!

Reading this book has been a pleasure; it is well written and carefully researched. It issues a clarion call to live a spirituality which is ideally suited to the post-modern age.

Roger and Chris approach the subject with humility, drawing on personal experiences and the experience of Revelation Church to illustrate how some of the lessons of the Celts can be earthed in our own lives. They are quick to acknowledge that they themselves are on a journey and some of the lessons of the journey provide significant moments of insight.

New Celts will no doubt be read by church leaders and those who already have an interest in Celtic spirituality. It is my hope that it will be read much more widely, for the lessons it contains are applicable for any who want to be followers of Christ.

Mike Pilavachi
March 1998

This book is dedicated to visionaries like Robert Wilder
(the Great Grandfather of Margaret Ellis)
who, alongside people like John Mott,
pioneered the Student Volunteer Movement
(the forerunner of SCM, IVF and UCCF),
saw 20,000 people inspired into world mission over two decades,
and first articulated the vision of evangelising the world
in one generation.

Their example is an inspiration to us.

Preface

This is a book written by two friends. We have been in
church leadership together in Revelation and across the
South Coast of England for an unbroken period of twelve
years. As such we have been through a lot together on the
roller-coaster of local church, and we appreciate what we
bring to one another's lives.

We are of one heart and vision on the subject of the
Celts, which has enabled us to write together. Yet we are
very different people in our gifts and perspectives, which
leads to a diversity in both style and content. We have
deliberately avoided a flattening out of these styles, and
hope that the reader can live with our differences.

Of course, such diversity is typically Celtic – carrying
the same flow of the Holy Spirit into the world but sometimes going in different directions!

Roger Ellis and Chris Seaton
Chichester 1998

Acknowledgements

We owe so much to so many friends who have stood alongside us as influencers and fellow adventurers.

We would like to thank Val Robinson for her tireless commitment to the typing of the manuscript. Ken Donald, Kath Fathers, Martin Goldsmith, Doug Heffernan, Roger Mitchell, Michael Mitton, Mike Pilavachi, Clive Price, Gary Pritchard, Martin Scott, and Andy Thornton for their encouragement, perspectives and corrections. The finished work has many imperfections but is all the better for their input!

Thanks also to our wonderful wives, Margaret Ellis and Charlotte Seaton for their partnership, care and love. This book is just the tip of the iceberg.

We dedicate this book to those individuals and communities who are committed participants in the 'Christ' adventure. In the words of many a football crowd, 'Here we go, here we go, here we go . . .'

Introduction

How can the church find its shape for the next millennium? What are the processes of study, understanding and revelation that need to occur to enable us to obey the Great Commission, captivate the emerging generations and transform society into the future?

We wish we could answer that question! However, this book represents a quest for answers, a hunger and a thirst for more of the living God, a deeper understanding of his word and a desire to learn from history. At the same time, we desire to engage creatively with the current spiritual milieu both within and outside the body of Christ.

Roots

There has recently been an explosion of interest in Celtic spirituality. This has ranged from pilgrimages to 'holy places' and unprecedented academic interest, to the stampede of *Riverdance* and *The Best Celtic Album in the World Ever*! This interest has been mirrored by some sections of the Christian church, which have begun to investigate their Celtic heritage. Perhaps there are many reasons why this is so, but here are two of them.

First, a millennial and *fin de siècle*[1] mood often causes people to look back to their roots. As far as the church is concerned, the year 1997 represented a remarkable anniversary, and the nation was reminded of its Christian ancestors by a set of commemorative postage stamps. Fourteen centuries ago, in 597, one of the greatest of the Celtic saints, Columba, died on Iona. In the same year Pope Gregory's special envoy, Augustine of Canterbury, landed on the Kent coast with a mission to convert the heathen Anglo-Saxons.

Second, the phenomenon known as post-modernity has taken a thorough grip on our culture in the nineties. Post-modernity challenges every certainty and every statement of accepted wisdom. This is particularly true of those certainties relating to the past three centuries that represent the values of the 'modern' world. The concepts of 'borrowing' and 're-inventing' have become more important than a quest for originality.

The worldview of the Celts is definitely 'pre-modern'. This isn't just because they lived before the days of cars, phones and Tupperware, but because the beliefs of their everyday lives were very different. Individualism as an ideology had not been invented. People saw themselves first of all as part of their community – family, clan, nation. There was an intrinsic spirituality and a ready belief in what we call 'the supernatural'. Celtic Christians were mystical and instinctively creative. They loved nature for its own sake, and saw God's fingerprints there.

Today more and more people seem to feel that these are values that have been lost along the way somewhere. Symbolism and image have become more attractive than the rather barren concepts of modernism. It's like those

---

[1] 'end of century'.

grey concrete statues of dead dictators in Eastern Europe that the people started pulling down after 1989. The population wanted an end to the concrete, the greyness and the tired ideas of state socialism. Perhaps the Celts represent some fresh colour, invention and texture after the beneficial but soulless ideas of technological progress, guaranteed security and material prosperity.

Today's church must wake up to appreciate that in the popular mind-set 'Christian' and 'modern' are often very closely linked. This is particularly true when we consider issues like environmentalism, where the church, unlike the Bible, has taken a completely non-spiritual approach to creation.

So, like strands of the knot beloved of Celtic artists, different factors have raised interest both in Celtic culture and in Celtic spirituality. One of the aims of this book is to examine the significance of the Celts, but to do so in a particular way.

A different approach

There are many excellent books on the market that take a look at the relevance of Celtic Christianity today, some of which are listed in the Bibliography. There have also been attempts to incarnate Celtic values in a number of communities established over recent years.[2] We have been greatly influenced and helped by many who have been involved with these projects and we honour their work. However, we are taking a somewhat different approach here as we look at the relevance of the Celts.

We believe that there is a strong sense of spiritual

---

[2] For example, the Order of St Aidan and St Hilda and the Northumbrian Community.

destiny about the British church at present. In the context of this season, a number of prophetic people have recently issued the call to 'dig wells'. Roger Mitchell was the first such prophet known to us, but this message seems to have been spoken in various parts of these islands, particularly in Wales and in Ireland.

The prophecy is based around Genesis 26:17–22. In this passage we read that Isaac not only dug fresh wells of life-giving water but he also re-opened the wells that had been dug by his father, Abraham. The latter had since been blocked by his enemy, the Philistines, to prevent Isaac from benefiting from his inheritance. The actions of Isaac served both to draw on the good work of his father, which had been capped and thus ceased to flow, and to pioneer something completely new.

The interpretation runs as follows. The Celtic saints are the 'Abraham' – the true aboriginal apostles – of Christianity in Britain today. They predate Roman Catholicism, Protestantism and all the radical movements as well. The 'wells' (the springs of Holy Spirit life) that they dug were meant to be for a flow of spiritual life from the Father that every subsequent generation of Christians could build upon. Instead, the wells have been blocked over the years through conflict, ecclesiastical imperialism and compromise.

We want to give attention to this message. To do so we must continue to pioneer new projects and plant new churches. We must dig new wells. We must also nurture values that have lain dormant, seek reconciliation between tribes, streams and movements that have grown separate, and pray over historic wounds. We must unblock the ancient wells.

Some see geography as unimportant. But it seems to us that the land plays a very significant role in a holistic biblical theology. In using 'holistic' we recognise that this term may be more readily associated by some with a New Age rather than Christian spirituality. However, we find it a useful means of describing a biblical approach that is integrated as opposed to one that might be described as 'dualistic' – that is, compartmentalised.

The first pioneers of the gospel in any nation seem to hold a key to the 'genetic code' of the church there. In Genesis 1:28–30 God sent humanity into the world in the first great commission, to create a diversity of culture interacting with him, with the landscape and with the creation around them. It's as if God placed rhythms in the earth itself which people were to explore and interpret with him.

Not that the Celts are important just because they were here first. Rather they laid unique, invaluable and truly biblical foundations in this land.

The first commission is expanded and deepened by Jesus in Matthew 28:16–20, where disciples are to be made of all nations. Consider the actions and beliefs of the first evangelists in any part of the world, whether nineteenth-century Europeans in Africa or seventeenth-century Puritans in America. You will see that their impact usually lasts for centuries. In the same way, our first evangelists, the Celtic church, should be honoured and explored.

Re-evangelisation

The Celtic Christians were the apostles and evangelists to what was basically a pagan Britain[3] and Ireland. Our age

---

[3] The term 'Britain' is used in this book in the strict sense of the largest island in the British Isles, comprised of England, Scotland and Wales.

is not only post-modern, it is also post-Christian. While this century's trend of 'negative church growth' began to be reversed in the 1980s, there are still hundreds of historic churches and denominations that are deeply in trouble. The message of the cross falls on deaf ears in a fractured generation that finds its packaging anachronistic and unattractive. Atheism might be a spent intellectual and spiritual force, but the ideas of New Age, Eastern mysticism and spiritual pluralism present a greater threat as they fight for the same territory as we do. The truth is no longer an undisputed reality to which we have to respond, but in the words of *The X Files* it's 'out there' – to be discovered and perhaps even invented for ourselves.

So our task is closely parallel to that presented to the great Celtic missions in Iona and Lindisfarne. Do we have the courage, faith and energy to transform a nation – to challenge and reshape its worldview? Will we let the wind of the Spirit fill our sails to take the good news to every corner of these lost islands? Will we let him lift our wings to fly beyond these shores to where God wants us to speak or bring a cup of water to those in need? Different centuries, same islands. Different ages, same challenge.

Our thesis

So the task of this book is not primarily one of historical research. We have sought to be as historically accurate as possible, recognising that the historicity of the Celtic church is a complicated matter. Its importance is a matter of great debate among the academic community. Because Celtic culture was not predominantly a written one, there is undoubtedly a mixture of fact and mythology in the records we have to hand.

Our approach to the history is that the Celtic church movement is a symbol to us. We acknowledge that there are myths involved, but believe firmly that there is a solid core of reality beneath them. In telling some of the stories, we hope not to seem naive or credulous, but we want to paint a picture of what the world looked like to the Celtic saints. Their stories reveal a wonderful world-view – of a God both with us and far above us, who is compassionate but uncompromising, affirming of life yet anything but worldly.

To put it another way, we are more concerned with the task of prophetically applying the Celtic themes to the coal-face of contemporary culture. We are not really interested in a beard-and-sandals nostalgia. This will not equip us effectively for the future. We are children of our techno culture, and an appeal to go back attracts us as little as it attracts young people today.

There is a tremendous temptation to over-romanticise the Celtic Christians. Their virtues are easily exalted. Yet we fully appreciate that they were a mixed bunch – like most other movements, including our own! Boniface, the English missionary so deeply influenced by Celtic Christianity, said he always smelled trouble when an Irish monk was around!

If it seems we are lionising them in these pages to an incredible extent, we are not trying to do so. When we generalise and refer to the 'Celtic church' we recognise that there is no single pristine example of this expression of church. However, we do make generalisations, seeking to pick up the heartbeat of Celtic Christianity. To qualify every positive statement about the Celts would be tedious reading indeed!

We make much of the distinction between the Roman and Celtic traditions. Again, there are generalisations made which refer to the broad sweep of events leading to and followed by the Synod of Whitby in 664. In being critical of the Roman tradition we are certainly not bashing what is now the Roman Catholic Church. The Roman/Celtic split predates the Reformation and the horrors of the Catholic/Protestant conflict of the past 400 years. Neither are we seeking to paint the divide as a black-and-white affair. Rather, it is the subjection of the Celts' uncomplicated creed and the rude beauty of their simple personal devotion to God, beneath Rome's pre-occupation with ecclesiastical power, that we are seeking to contrast.

Which brings us to the method we use to build a bridge between the historical Celtic Christians and our contemporary Christian lives. We use the phrase 'New Celts' to describe a strong sense of identification with the Celts. On our journey we have found the original Celtic church to be a *leitmotiv*, a recurring theme in the plot, as we live our lives on a different stage. As we say, we are not advocating a 'go retro' reversion to the *form* of sixth-century Christianity in the British Isles. Rather we are proposing that there is a baton we need to pick up if we are to be effective in the re-evangelisation of these islands. This is what unblocking the wells means to us.

By using Celtic Christianity and Roman Christianity as types and symbols in this way, we can see how the Roman mind-set has continued to manifest itself in most of the streams down to contemporary Christianity. How easy it is to find in church life a top-down, hierarchical institution dominated by an all-male clerical élite, far too concerned about wealth and political influence.

To be a New Celt is to engage with post-modern ideas by borrowing from our aboriginal apostles. Seeking to hear their voices and pick up their heartbeat, we pray that through our borrowing and reinterpreting we might find ourselves better equipped to re-evangelise our generation.

1

Who Were the Celts?

In this chapter we want to give some background to our theme. To draw meaningful lessons from the Celtic church we need to have some understanding of what that church was like. In turn, to be able to understand the brand of Christianity that emerged among the Celts requires that we have some idea of who the Celts were. We will do this in three brief sketches examining Celtic origins, what the Celts were like and what they believed. In a few hundred words there is not space to do these subjects justice. These sketches aim simply to give a flavour of who the Celts were. The Bibliography gives references for anyone wishing to delve more deeply.

The early traces

While the origins of the Celts are still shrouded in many mysteries, they have an established place of significance in the history of Europe. They are the first great nation north of the Alps whose name is known.

Perhaps it would be more accurate to say 'whose names are known'. The Celts were not a highly organised nation in the modern sense, but a cluster of tribes sharing many common cultural and linguistic ties. These tribes were often in conflict and seem to have been highly migratory. Many of the names of the Celtic tribes are still familiar today: the *Galli* of Gaul, the *Belgae* of north-eastern Gaul and the *Galatae* of Galatia in Asia Minor. Manchester United fans surely can't forget the modern incarnation of this tribe in the form of the Turkish football team, *Galatasaray*! Strangely enough, the only place where the name of a tribe known as *Celtici* survived to Roman times was in south-western Spain.

This loose-knit barbaric Celtic nation came into being in central Europe some time after 1000 BC. The oldest surviving reference to it is rather brief and casual. The Greek writer, Herodotus, mentions the *Keltoi* in passing in the mid-fifth century BC when writing about the source of the River Danube. The way he mentions them suggests that they were a people already known to the Greeks. It seems that at this time Celtic people stretched from the Upper Danube region round to northern Portugal.

During the fifth and fourth centuries BC the Celts reached their prominence. They migrated south into Italy and the Balkans, west to Iberia, east to Asia Minor and north to the mouth of the Rhine and across to the British Isles. Our two main islands were known then to the Greeks as *Ierne* (Ireland) and *Albion* (Britain). The dominant Celtic tribes of these islands were the *Preteni*, later mispronounced *Britanni* (the root word of 'Britannia') by Julius Caesar. We do not know much about the people, if there were any, who lived in these islands before the arrival of the Celts. What is clearer is that the first Celts to arrive here did so in the early eighth century. BC

Mention of Julius Caesar brings us to the period of the decline of the Celts. As any *aficionado* of the *Asterix* cartoons will know, it was his campaigns that brought Celtic independence to an end. With the pacification by the Romans came ethnic mixing and this was followed by the virtual eradication of the Celts on the continent. Eventually the only survivors of the once widespread nation were the groups of tribes in the west of Britain (like the *Cimri*), the north of Britain (like the *Picti*) and in Ireland (like the *Scoti*). In fact, only in Ireland did there survive a language, and literature, that sprang directly from the ancient Celts, uncontaminated by Imperial Rome. As we shall see, this is of great importance when we consider the development of what is called Celtic Christianity.

What were the Celts like?

There are a number of accounts in Greek and Latin literature of the striking physical appearance of the Celts. Some remarked on the terrifying sight of a charge of well-built Gaulish warriors. Others noted their height, fair skin, muscularity, blue eyes and blond hair. This may not sound like our usual idea of, say, a Gaelic or a Welsh Celt today, but clearly there was great physical diversity within this loose 'race' of people.

At the Battle of Telamon (225 BC), some of the Gaulish invaders wore trousers and light cloaks. The *Gaesatae*, on the other hand, would parade their fighting men naked except for gold torcs (neck-rings) and armlets! Some warriors would wear long moustaches and smear their hair back with a wash of lime to produce a weird effect like the mane of a horse. In Irish texts there are references to long stiff hair that would have been capable of impaling falling apples. In one, the hair is described as being in three colours, darkest near the scalp and lightest at the extremities, with an intermediate colour in between.

Maybe highlights are not so original!

Remarkably, there is evidence on a statue of a pair of tartan-patterned trousers on a Briton who was brought as a slave to Rome (prefiguring the more dubiously Celtic Bay City Rollers of the 1970s?). The tunics of the Celtic nobles were dyed and embroidered, and their coloured cloaks were fastened with a brooch. The Celts loved ornaments: neck-rings of gold were the most characteristic, but also bronze head-rings were worn by women, and bracelets, finger-rings and brooches were worn by all but slaves.

When they weren't fighting, the Celts were agricultural people, busily involved in mixed farming for their own food production. Socially they were divided into *tuath* (to use the Irish word) or tribes. Within these tribes there was usually a king, then nobles, free commoners and finally slaves. Within each *tuath* the most important social unit was the kin or *fine*. Land was not held by an individual but by a kinship group, showing the paramount importance of the concept of community to the Celts.

The Celts' strong links with the land gave them an intense sense of the spirituality of nature. As we shall see later, this sometimes arose from a fear of the consequences of disease and failing harvests. Yet there is also evidence, particularly within Irish literature, that the Celts appreciated and loved the natural world.

But what about the spirit of the Celts? Strabo, a Roman writer from second century BC, described them as being 'war-mad, and both high-spirited and quick for battle although otherwise simple and not uncouth'. These few words seem to express the image gained by the Celts as a living and colourful people. Other qualities described are personal bravery – even recklessness – on the battlefield, yet hospitality and etiquette in the home. In contrast to the excitability and passion of the Celts, there is also evidence of a sense of responsibility and duty within a well-defined social system. The love of bright colours, ornamentation, praise and entertainment, feasting and quarrelling has been carried down into our current understanding of the Celtic spirit.

What did the Celts believe?

'Celtic spirituality' has become one of those phrases that is guaranteed to make people sit up and listen. Unfortunately, the vast majority of so-called Celtic material that one finds on bookshelves and at Internet websites is anything but Christian in character. Much of this material can be of a rather sinister, sometimes occultic and always extremely pagan nature. Indeed there are quite a number within the ranks of the evangelical constituency who have been very keen to point this fact out to us!

So this provides a double reason why we should have some familiarity with Celtic primitive religion: first, to understand the spiritual context into which the gospel originally came; and second because of the renewed interest in that pagan Celtic spirituality that we currently find to be all around us.

The first thing to be clear on is that when we talk of a pre-Christian Celtic spirituality, we are simply talking about an animistic 'old religion'. It would be very wrong to think in terms of a clear-cut body of belief or a consistent view about such subjects as life after death or humanity's relationship with the supernatural. T. G. E. Powell makes the point that, with the Celts, it is more accurate to talk in terms of an obsession with magic and the observance of ritual than of a religion as we understand it.[1]

---

[1] T. G. E. Powell, *The Celts,* p. 143.

When looking at Celtic beliefs and practices, you notice that in common with many other animistic faiths there is a strong element of being aware of something bigger 'out there'. Because of the technological revolutions – of agriculture, science, industry and communication – which have visited us over the past three centuries, we so easily forget what it must have been like to feel at the mercy of the natural world. Crops could fail through flood, drought or blight. People and livestock alike could perish through disease, wild animals and the violence of an enemy. Thus, in an age-old tradition going back to their Neolithic ancestors, the Celts treated the supernatural world as something to be regarded with fear and to be kept at a distance where possible. At best the powers of magic were to be constrained to a positive end by placating the gods with sacrifices and rituals.

When it is looked at in this way, Celtic paganism loses some of its romantic mystique. Certainly when we talk about rituals, human sacrifice was undoubtedly heavily involved. Fertility rites sometimes included the sacrifice to the nature goddess of a man from each kinship community. Caesar notes how some Gaulish tribes made great wickerwork constructions, filled them with living victims (preferably wrongdoers) and set the whole lot alight to ensure tribal welfare.

Another case is of a terrifying three-faced god whose anger was propitiated by the death of three victims – one by drowning, one by hanging and one by burning. Gruesome stuff, but consistent with the sort of primitive rituals discovered by Christian missionaries in Africa, America and Asia in more recent centuries.

The ritual calendar was very important to the Celts, and the most important festival was *Samain*. In the modern calendar this would fall on 1 November, but then it would have been New Year's Day; that is, the separation of the two main seasons: warm and cold. Once again, we see how it ties in with the pastoral seasons, the time when flocks and herds are gathered for the winter. But its magical significance was that *Samain* was the time to ensure the renewal of earthly prosperity and tribal success. In other words, it was the season to sow good luck that they hoped would be reaped the following spring and summer!

On *Samain* the Celts' most powerful god, Dagda, was united with Morrigan, Queen of Demons. She occurs frequently in Irish writings and her name can be interchanged with other rather unattractive ones like Panic, Raven of Battle and Mare. These were the spiritual forces to be placated at *Samain*. Indeed, the paganism of contemporary Hallowe'en harks back to the idea that the night before *Samain* was the great occasion in the year when the material world was overrun by forces of magic.

Yet alongside these disastrous practices and images can be found more positive examples of the kind of pre-Christian ideas that also occur in other primitive religions. For example, Patrick found that some tribes had within their local deity, gods named Eternal Father and Sacrificial Son. What's more, many of the Celtic gods were triplistic, although not Trinitarian. This concept contains the idea of the great potency of a god or goddess who was three and one. Three was therefore a sacred number that goes to explain why the Celtic Christians loved to invoke the Trinity, or 'the name of the powerful three'.

Finally, mention must be made of the magicians and sages of the Celts, the Druids. As with other aspects of Celtic paganism, the modern romantic fiction of the role of the Druids amounts to little more than 'cod druidism'.

Most historians would argue that the Druid has much in common with Brahmins of India and the shaman of North Eurasia and North America. One of the distinctives of the Celts was that the druidic class was recruited from the children of the aristocracy.

One aspect which does seem to fit their modern image is the fact that the Druid was versed in an understanding of the spirituality of nature. Indeed the word 'Druid' is thought to suggest 'knowledge of the oak' (the oak being the symbol of deity among trees). Druids, along with other Celtic learned magicians like the bards and the ecstatic prophets and poets, held the keys to the supernatural. Their power lay in their ability to see the invisible and to use that invisible power to impact the temporal world. This was usually achieved through frenzy and trance.

Once again, there is an important link here between this context of Celtic paganism and the up-front supernatural evangelism of Patrick, Columba and others. These evangelists were not coming to a situation without any experience of spiritual power, but to a culture where the pagan forces had to be contested and unmasked. Truly it took Celtic evangelists to rise to this task.

The way in which these evangelists did this will be the subject of the next chapter.

Trinity

2

The Great Divide

Wells, streams and the river

As we hinted in the Introduction, in considering the history of Celtic Christianity we want to do more than sketch out a narrative of people and events. (Some of the historical headlines are set out in an overview in Appendix 1.) Rather, we are more interested in telling their story in big brush-strokes as an exercise in 'well-digging'. The wells they dug produced streams of Christian life and 'anointing',[1] some of which have become dried up, and are waiting to be rediscovered.

Having said this, the spread of the Christian faith through these islands is due not just to one, but to the presence of three streams of witness between the fifth and eighth centuries. These three streams may vary in their quality and their impact, but each contributes to achieve the effective christianisation (if not the complete evangelisation) of these islands.

---

[1] By using 'anointing' in this context we mean a particular sense of the Holy Spirit's presence and power to fulfil a task. Biblically, this phrase refers to the oil of anointing for office, used, for example, on kings and prophets in the Old Testament.

The first stream is that of the ancient British church,[2] a remnant of the days of the original Roman occupation. We will argue here that this stream was more Celtic than anything else, and that it anticipates the second stream we will describe. Unfortunately, these Christians took a terrible battering during the Saxon invasions of the fifth century. Finally, the Saxons drove them to the western and northern extremities of Britain and beyond.

The second stream is that of the main thrust of Celtic Christianity, beginning in Ireland and coming to Great Britain with Columba via Iona. All these strands had their own distinctive qualities, although by the eighth century each had more or less become interwoven with the others. Therefore to separate the purely Celtic from this time onwards becomes difficult.

The third stream is the Gregorian Mission led by Augustine of Canterbury in 596/7 – the 'official' date of the conversion of England. This saw the formal introduction of the Roman church and accounted for the christianisation of what is now England.

The psalmist says, 'There is a river whose streams make glad the city of God, the holy place where the Most High dwells' (Ps 46:4). In creation, the confluence of different streams gives greater power, depth and energy to a river. The mighty Zambezi River is a stream you can paddle across near its source in north-western Zambia. By the time it reaches the Kariba Dam so many tributaries have swelled the river that the power of its flow has been harnessed to provide much of the nation's electricity.

---

[2] The descriptions 'British' and 'Britain' when used in connection with this period refer to the island of Great Britain, the largest of the British Isles. We should try to read it without the contemporary political overtones of the Celtic/English conflicts.

Just so, there is something about the flowing together of spiritual streams of anointing that works towards the strengthening and deepening of a move of God in a nation. We can apply this principle to contemporary 'wells' with which we are familiar. The streams of revival from the wells of Toronto in Canada, Pensacola in Florida and Argentina in South America have flowed into our nation across many denominational boundaries in recent years. Likewise, there have been tools like Alpha, Cities for God and March for Jesus that have either stimulated or been enhanced by local church unity. Many have experienced blessing in their towns and cities where different churches have found grace to meet across their divides to pray, to worship and to witness.

One of the <u>central ideas</u> of this book is that it was the failure of the confluence of the ancient streams in these islands that led to the waning of the vigour of the church here by the ninth century. When we reach the tenth century we can see the complete subjugation of Celtic spirituality beneath Rome, an end to missionary endeavour and the presence of a rigid, hierarchical parish system. Something went wrong somewhere.

We <u>also</u> believe that this dividing of ancient streams has contributed to the tensions that have existed ever since between the English and the Celtic nations. Many have commented that these islands may well have been very different if the Celtic/Roman conflict had gone in a different direction. We pick up this theme fully in Chapter 9.

For now, we want to look at the reasons for this great divide, paying particular attention to the Celtic Christians. We hope to learn from them and to try to discover how their immense contribution was absorbed and subverted.

Early apostles

Before picking up the story of the conversion of the Celts in Ireland, the 'heartland' of Celtic Christianity, we turn our attention to the first of these wells: the ancient British church in *Albion* or Great Britain. Historians hotly debate the extent of Christianity in Roman Britain. There is even dispute about whether it was the Romans who first brought the gospel to these islands. Some have argued that it could have been a strong and healthy grass-roots movement. Others, like Murray, have suggested that Britain probably turned gradually to nominal Christianity as did other parts of the Roman Empire.[3]

 The accepted line until recently has been that it was converted Roman legionaries and civil servants who brought the faith to these islands as they were posted here. If this was the case, then the common Celtic peoples of Britain would generally have associated Christianity with the ruling classes of Rome. This scenario would lend itself to the theory of a nominal church. It would also explain Christianity's rapid decline in what is now England after the retreat of the Roman legions in 410.

In complete contrast to this account is the well-known legend of Joseph of Arimathea. The story has it that, as well as being a member of the Sanhedrin and an established elder in Israel, Joseph was also a renowned tin trader. His trade would have taken him to the West of Britain, where he is supposed to have made several visits after the death of Jesus. The wilder versions of the legend even have the Lord Jesus himself travelling to Britain with Joseph before he began his public ministry. It was this

---

[3] Stuart Murray, *A Loser's Guide to Church History*, p. 29.

myth that inspired William Blake to ponder, 'And did those feet in ancient time walk upon England's mountains green?' in his patriotic poem-turned-hymn, 'Jerusalem'. From here the Holy Grail and other Arthurian legends sprang up. Is all this pure fantasy? It is clearly a story-telling legend, but there might perhaps be a grain of truth in the suggestion of the gospel's arrival in *Albion* from this route.

While there is nothing other than circumstantial evidence to suggest that Joseph himself brought the gospel (let alone the Holy Grail!) to Britain, it is certainly true that there was a vigorous trade route between the Eastern Mediterranean and the British Isles. What's more, the great Tertullian of Carthage in 210 wrote of 'regions of Briton inaccessible to the Romans but subject to Christ'. These clues raise serious doubts about whether the first British apostles, and indeed the first real evangelists to Britain, were Roman.

Not surprisingly, it is possible to find support for this idea among Celtic writers. In the sixth century the Welsh bard, Taliesin, wrote: 'Christ the Word was from the beginning our Teacher, and we never lost his teaching.'[4] Higham interprets another Welshman, the enigmatic Gildas, to be hinting strongly that the masses of the conquered Celtic Britons were indeed true Christians by the time of the departure of the Romans.[5] The implications of this possibility are profound. It would mean that, although there were undoubtedly many good Christian Romans in Britain before 410 (indeed the first known British martyr, Alban, was Romano–British), the most

---

4 As quoted in Ian Bradley, *The Celtic Way,* p. 6.
5 N. Higham, *The English Conquest I: Gildas and Britain in the Fifth Century.*

ancient of the roots of Christianity in these islands are
essentially non-Roman.

East goes West

So if the first serious evangelists in Britain did not come
here from Rome, where did they come from? There is
always the possibility that the gospel spread direct from
Jerusalem shortly after Pentecost, but again we find no
firm indications of this. However, it does seem clear that
there was a strong influence upon the early native
Christian community in these islands from the 'desert
fathers' of Egypt, Palestine and Syria. It was these ascetic
believers[6] who launched the worldwide monastic movement by leaving their towns and cities to live the hermit's
harsh life of bodily denial, contemplation and prayer.

We know there were trade routes between Alexandria (in
Egypt) and Constantinople (the present Istanbul) and the
British Isles via Gibraltar and the Bay of Biscay. For
example, it has been shown that British minerals were being
traded for wine in Tintagel and for pottery in Glastonbury
in the fourth and fifth centuries. It is assumed that these
routes were forged around the time of Julius Caesar.

It is significant that this Eastern influence is expressed
throughout mainstream Celtic Christianity. For example,
Bradley has drawn comparisons between the Christian
artwork found in Ireland and Wales and that found in
the Caucasus mountains.[7] He likens the illustrations in

---

6 The dictionary definition of an ascetic is 'one who rigidly denies
   himself ordinary bodily gratifications for conscience' sake: one who
   aims to compass holiness through mortification of the flesh'
   (Chambers).
7 Bradley, *The Celtic Way*, p. 10.

women

the Book of Kells to the icons found in Egyptia[n] Coptic churches. Other scholars have even argued the design of the Celtic knot is borrowed from the Eastern Mediterranean. Perhaps more fundamentally than this, the Celtic church followed the Eastern traditions of the dating of Easter and baptismal formula. Notably, these were the presenting issues that brought the Celtic/Roman conflict to a head, both at Aust and finally at the Synod of Whitby.

These are merely signposts that point us towards an important ingredient in early Celtic Christianity: its spiritual and cultural origin. One of the fascinating things about the Celtic wells was that they were dug with the rigid discipline of the desert fathers but were mixed with a life-affirming worldview. They loved life and celebration, but they did not indulge their bodies. They were less *NOTE* marred than the Roman church by the dualistic influence of the ancient Greek philosopher, Plato. It was Augustine of Hippo's neoplatonism that taught the rigid separation of the spiritual and the material worlds and which casts such a long shadow across the landscape of Western thinking.

In contrast, the worldview of the Celts was remarkably holistic. The Celts were passionate, adventurous and full of wandering, yet their Eastern-influenced spirituality also gave them a great appetite for meditation, Scripture and seeking God. It is this unique spiritual 'genetic code', reflected in our aboriginal apostles, which resonates so strongly with us today.

So the Celtic 'stream' probably arrived here direct from the Near East or from North Africa. If this is so, then it would have had more in common with the mainstream Celtic church that was to follow than its Roman counterpart. The well of the ancient British church might even have been established in these islands within a few decades of the resurrection of Christ. The flow of this stream can only be described as shadowy as far as we know, yet possibly it was strong and very significant in parts. Indeed, perhaps it has laid deep foundations in the spiritual structures of our land. Unfortunately, there is an almost complete lack of source material for what went on during the Roman occupation, making it hard to back up such thoughts.

However, the reason why it remains so unknown after the departure of the Romans is much clearer. We mentioned above that the first British church might have declined rapidly because of its close association with the occupying forces, but there is also a more simple explanation. This ancient church, along with the original British Celts – the *pretani* people – was swept away by the arrival of the Teutonic hoards from 428 onwards. As Gildas called them, 'the ferocious Saxons (name not to be spoken!), hated by man and God . . .'.[8] The Saxons were not popular with the Celts. Quotations like this, and accounts of the brutality of the Saxon invaders, render it easy to see why there was little enthusiasm among the Celts for evangelising the new occupants of southern Britain.

Gospel meets Celt

So we turn to pick up the story of the second of the three streams to touch these islands: the Celtic Christian movement as it is best known to us, from western Britain and Ireland.

Before we go further, let us say a word about the use

---

[8] Gildas, *De Excidio Brittonum* (The Ruin of Britain).

of historical materials. Our view of the shape of Celtic Christianity has been profoundly influenced by the work of historians like Gildas (fifth and sixth century) and Bede of Jarrow (673–735). Bede in particular was a compiler and relied heavily upon earlier sources, which in most cases were the disciples of the men and women whose lives they were describing. Thus, one of the eternal challenges in drawing a clear picture of Celtic Christianity is to strip back the myths, legends and other elaborations to expose the truth.

Having said this, one of the results of the trend of demythologising Bede and others has been the discounting of his innumerable accounts of the supernatural. These include healings, words of knowledge, words of wisdom and many other signs and wonders. While appreciating the concerns of these critics, we must distance ourselves from a purely rationalistic approach and conclude that there was in Celtic Christianity much that charismatics and Pentecostals would recognise today.

Increasingly, historians are beginning to acknowledge that the growing body of evidence for miracles occurring today must influence their view of the Celts' accounts of miracles. As Ian Finlay says, 'We should be foolish to dismiss as mere eulogy Columba's saintly powers of healing the genuinely sick . . . There is abundant evidence today of spiritual healing.'[9]

As we look at the earliest names among the Celtic saints, we see an interesting mixture of both the Eastern connection and the Roman stream. For example, Ninian, the very first British Christian Celt whom we can certainly identify, probably received his theological education in Rome. Yet when he founded his monastery in Whithorn

---

[9] Ian Finlay, *Columba*.

(Strathclyde), he dedicated it to Martin of Tours. This suggests he might have also studied under Martin in Gaul. The pioneering monasteries of this Gallic bishop are the first to be founded in Western Europe and, once again, clearly owe a lot to the influence of the desert fathers.

Some have argued that Gaul was the seedbed of Celtic Christianity. While there is little concrete evidence for this, there are those who have suggested that there was a major growth spurt in the fifth century due to the influx of refugee monks from Gaul fleeing persecution after the departure of the Romans. Others would hotly dispute this, claiming that it was simply the energy and effort of Patrick that led to such dramatic church growth.

It is during the period of the fifth century that we can find the clearest evidence of the Eastern stream of Christianity influencing the Celtic church. There are some extraordinary examples of this influence. One is a standing cross in Ireland that bears the image of a species of fish found only in Egyptian waters. Another is the evidence of Welsh liturgies that contain the sayings of famous Egyptian desert fathers. But the influence was not only one way. The British monk, Pelagius, travelled to North Africa and Palestine to work out his affirmative doctrine of humanity that his followers developed into Pelagianism – an unhelpful heresy. Meanwhile the monk himself was following a strand of thought (bringing him into great conflict with Rome) which many of us today find more constructive than some of Augustine's doctrinal ideas.

So, we turn our attention back to Ireland. Whatever the extent and the quality of the ancient British church under Roman occupation, it seems that Ireland – beyond the Empire – remained quite unevangelised. When Patrick (and possibly the Gallic refugee monks) brought their Christianity to Ireland, they found that it was still pretty much the last bastion of the pagan Celtic world as we described it in Chapter 1. The early Irish Christians were still loyal to the Roman church, but they certainly carried a different flow and they contributed to the digging of a very distinct well.

The world they encountered is significant because it was unique at that time. When the Roman church began to re-evangelise the early Teutonic kingdoms of continental Europe from the sixth century onwards, the missionaries found only the most basic structures of law and social order to be in place. In contrast, in Ireland there was a highly developed body of learned people, with specialists in sacred arts, heroic literature and genealogy. The culture in the fifth century was pre-literate, but this was not necessarily a disadvantage as phenomenal powers of memory were developed. No wonder the Roman officials would have Druids educate their children!

These skills were brought into the life of the Christian disciple. Part of the basic training of an Irish monk was to learn the Book of Psalms by heart. More 'Latin' learning was grafted into this wisdom over the following centuries. As Powell puts it:

> Paganism alone was supplanted, and the traditional oral schools continued to flourish, but now side by side with the monasteries. By the seventh century, if not earlier, there existed aristocratic Irish monks who had also been fully educated in the traditional native learning. This led to the first writing-down of the vernacular literature, which thus became the oldest in Europe next after Greek and Latin.[10]

----

[10] Powell, *The Celts,* p. 57.

In this quotation we find another key to the rich unique-
ness of Celtic Christianity. Patrick and the other missionaries to Ireland brought the gospel, but they did not
impose the culture they brought. Maybe this was because
of the diversity of the backgrounds of the earliest evangelists – Gallic, Roman,[11] Egyptian and so on. Maybe it was
because the majority of them were coming from decaying
cultures to a still-vibrant culture.

Whatever the reason, Powell's observation is profound
in that it helps us to understand the Celts as quite excep-
tional in their approach to culture. This is brought out
beautifully in Thomas Cahill's rollicking history, *How the
Irish Saved Civilisation*.[12] He claims that to caricature the
Irish Celts simply as wild and passionate beings does no
justice to their commitment to learning. Because of this
commitment, hundreds of monks spent their lives
copying out the texts of antiquity, not only in Britain, but
in the monasteries of Europe. If you are familiar with Sean
Connery's back catalogue, you might recall this theme
came out in the film *The Name of the Rose*.

Unlike their Roman counterparts, the Celts resisted the
temptation to demonise and destroy every idea that did
not square with their particular view of the world. Perhaps
this is one of the keys to their missionary success: the ability
to appreciate other cultures and to use some of the wisdom
in these cultures to tell the gospel story. This approach
endured to the eighth century, reaching on through to the
achievements of Boniface, the apostle to the Germans.

The Celtic approach to culture raises once again the

---

[11] An example of this is that around 430 Pope Celestine I sent out a
   priest called Palladius to act as Bishop to the Irish (probably because
   he wanted some control over them!).

[12] Doubleday, New York, 1996.

women 45

question of worldview – one that is absolutely v...
understanding of the Celtic/Roman conflict th...
lowed. This approach probably stems from Pat...k's
embracing of the Irish during the spiritual training in the
wilderness of his slavery. The foundation laid by the Holy
Spirit became the bedrock for the future understanding
and synthesis that marked the writings of the monks and
the wild missions of the Irish saints.

The Romans[13] showed little love for the natural world
and appear to have viewed it, like Plato before them, as a
prison in which the soul is trapped. Celtic hymns and
poems celebrate the Creator of what we now describe
separately as the natural and the supernatural worlds. As
a ninth-century Irish poet writes:

> Let us adore the Lord,
> Maker of wondrous works,
> Great bright heaven with its angels,
> The white-waved sea on the earth.[14]

In contrast, Roman worship of this period is far more
interested in the inner life of the soul.

Another interesting example of this worldview clash is in
the area of sexuality. Some Celtic priests and monks
married, and some were celibate.[15] However, even the celibate men appear to have retained a positive view of women.
Patrick delights to write about 'a blessed woman, Irish by
birth, noble, extraordinarily beautiful – a true adult – whom
I baptised'. On the other hand, the Neoplatonic worldview

---

[13] From here on the description 'Roman' is applied to the expression
of Western Christianity rather than to the old Empire of Rome.

[14] G. Murphy (ed.), *Early Irish Lyrics*, p. 5

[15] In the same way, there were single-sex monasteries and also mixed
houses. The most remarkable example of the latter was Whitby
Abbey where a woman, Hilda, was Abbess.

produced not only asceticism, but often misogyny as well! For example, Augustine of Canterbury describes a woman's embrace as 'sordid, filthy and horrible'.

As we tie these strands together we can thus grasp the fact that in Ireland a rather unique well of Christianity was dug. It is this that we have come to know as Celtic Christianity.

The Celts and the gospel

In tracing the story we can see that the link between Ireland and Britain was very important. There is evidence of strong evangelistic work from Whithorn, and also that it was used as a training centre by Irish monks. Other Irish monks travelled to Illtyd's monastery in South Wales. Of course, mainland Britain also gave Ireland its patron saint and the first great hero of the Celtic church, Patrick.

Born somewhere in the west of Britain around 390, Patrick was a captive in Ireland when he found faith in Christ. An Irishman has described his preparation in Ireland in this way:

It was here with the pigs and in atrocious conditions that Patrick learned from God alone. These circumstances were his Bible College. He only developed his intellectual knowledge later in the hope of getting approval from his peers. He came to Ireland as a slave and a nominal Christian but he left the island totally changed. Here he learned the nature of prayer and a love for a people who were not his own people. Out on the wind-swept hills in all weathers he encountered a God who answered prayer powerfully. Many a night he must have cursed his captors and hated God and the Irish. During his Spirit training he learned the power of *peregrinatio pro Christo*, separation to God alone.

We have to look back to Patrick to understand the whole

nature of *peregrinatio* because it stems not only from the mission of Martin of Tours but also from the Irish culture that he encountered. This culture already had a developed understanding of exile both within and without Ireland. Patrick's emphasis on dependence on God alone no doubt sowed the seeds of independence from Roman control that forever after marked everything he did for God. He also learned to love his enemies, imbibing their culture. It was here that the seeds of true evangelism were sown in his heart. Turning the Irish people to God would not be a domination process. It was a process of embracing all that was good and wholesome in the Irish culture and a process of promoting the biblical God, the God of Creation and the Eternal Son, through the power of the Holy Spirit. Patrick's view of mission may have been further reinforced by Martin of Tours (and his mission to the pagans) through an exposure to continental streams and no doubt Martin was a leading Apostle of the time.[16]

After leaving Ireland, Patrick spent some time in Gaul. During this period he was trained, either in Rome as some traditions suggest, or in the Mediterranean island of Lerins referred to in his *Confessions*. Lerins was known as a centre 'where monks from the Near East thronged' and was held in some suspicion by Rome. Once again, we find the Eastern flow being mixed into Celtic roots.

He received what might be termed a 'Macedonian call' (see Acts 16:9) to return to Ireland around 432. Basing himself in the Armagh area, he proceeded to evangelise the Irish with a mixture of zealous preaching, miraculous signs and persuasion of the chieftains. Patrick rightfully holds a pre-eminent role as a founding father in the history of the Celtic church. After thirty years of ministry he had established a nationwide church organised by diocese. However, it seems that alongside this a network

---

[16] Doug Heffernan, in personal correspondence, 11 January 1998.

of monasteries rapidly emerged in the sixth and seventh centuries. These were to have a greater impact on the development of the church in Ireland than the Roman-style parochial system.

Alongside the development of the monasteries in the early Irish church the concept of Celtic mission was also developed. Far from twentieth-century ideas of strategies for growth and mission, the Celtic saints would talk of going 'on a pilgrimage'. *Peregrinatio*, as it is termed in Latin, was the single-minded search for God on this earth. It might involve the life of a hermit in his cell or a wandering on foot. Most frequently *peregrinatio* led to exile in a foreign land – anything to be free of earthly ties and thus be more free for God. It was this somewhat other-worldly approach, rather than an express desire to preach to and convert pagans, that prompted the apparently bizarre journeys of those like Brendan, Dubslane and Macbethu. Naturally, as opportunity presented itself or where the lifestyle proved attractive, these saints would delight in sharing the gospel. However, one cannot help but conclude that evangelism was often an unplanned by-product of godly personal devotion.

One of the shortest yet most far-reaching, the journey of Columba (521–597)[17] and his twelve colleagues to the tiny island of Iona, was just such a *peregrinatio*. Its results were to have a profound and lasting effect. Although Mayr-Harting suggests that it was partly in order to establish his own security on Iona, Columba – a gentle yet powerful man and a severe ascetic – went on to convert King Brude of the Picts. It is unclear how much of western Scotland he personally covered, but the work of his monks certainly led to the founding of many

---

[17] Columba is more widely known in Ireland as Columcille.

monasteries. The well dug at Iona was perhaps the most
important of all and Iona itself became established as one
of the greatest missionary centres of the Celtic church.
Built on the site of an old Druid temple, the monastery
grew to house about 150 monks. From here came the
evangelists who effectively converted most of what is now
Scotland and northern England.

Columba is recorded as engaging in a number of
Mount Carmel-type confrontations (see 1 Kings 18) with
pagan priests and he left behind him a tradition of real and
simple sanctity. His biographer, Adamnan, wrote: 'In the
midst of all his cares he showed himself open and friendly
to everyone; he bore the joy of the Holy Spirit in the
inmost place of his heart.'[18] He was also the power behind
the idea of abbot-rule as distinct from bishop-rule. This
major distinctive of the Celtic church, the subjugation of
the bishop, must have become a poke in the eye to the
Romans and a clear line marking out the parties.

But there was also another side to Columba. He was a
gifted politician, being involved as something of a king-
maker in the formation of the new Irish kingdom of
Dalraida in western Scotland. In a society where tribal
loyalty was so powerful, involvement in the murky waters
of politics was not something Columba felt he should be
above. This fact points us to another key in the success of
the Celts. Again, the modern word 'holistic' comes to
mind when one reads back into their approach to society.
While there remained an emphasis on solitude, the monks
also adapted themselves to their surrounding culture –
being very much 'in' the world around them. Columba's
connection with royalty and the power games of contemporary Britain was one example of this.

---

[18]   Quoted in Neill, *A History of Christian Missions*, p. 60.

Indeed, it was due to the fact that Iona had this level of profile that the door to England opened in the first place. Prince Oswald of Northumbria had visited the island as a refugee around 617. During his stay he was converted and baptised there, and on becoming king he requested of the Abbot of Iona that someone be sent to evangelise his people. It was Aidan who went to Northumbria with a band of monks and there they founded the monastery of Lindisfarne. Soon this became a centre for evangelising the Northumbrians and the rest of the border country. It was from here that the major missions to the Anglo-Saxon kingdoms of Mercia and Essex were later launched.

Lindisfarne was another wonderful Celtic well. But its founding takes us beyond 597 and so we will leave the Celts here to turn to look at the final stream – that of Pope Gregory's mission to the Anglo-Saxons.

Before doing so it should be said that the real draw of the Celtic Christians for us is not primarily an appreciation of their considerable achievements for the gospel, impressive as they are. It is more to do with their complex personalities, their gentle and integrated way of life, their mixture of humanity and austerity and the colour they used to express their faith. We borrow and concur with the words of Dr Chadwick who claims that they express 'the Christian ideal with a sanctity and a sweetness which has never been surpassed'.[19] This ideal was captured beautifully in one of Bede's most famous passages. It is a quotation from a speech made by an unnamed member of the King's Council when King Edwin of Northumbria was debating with his nobles in 627 whether they should accept Christianity.

---

[19] From the Introduction of Nora Chadwick's *The Age of Saints in the Early Celtic Church*.

The present life of man, oh King, seems to me, in comparison with that time which is unknown to us, like the swift
flight of a sparrow through the room in which you sit at
supper in winter around the fire while the wind is howling
and the snow is drifting without. It passes swiftly in at one
door and out through another, feeling for the moment the
warmth of shelter of your palace; but it flies from winter to
winter and swiftly escapes from our sight. Even such is our
life here, and if anyone can tell us certainly what lies beyond
it, we shall do wisely to follow his teaching.

The fact that the Celtic evangelists spoke into this context
so effectively reminds us of their lasting value and
achievements.

The third stream: the Roman mission

Becoming Bishop of Rome in 590, Pope Gregory the
Great is generally recognised as one of the church's most
significant leaders of the period known as the Dark Ages.
He held enormous power, as effective imperial authority
in Rome had all but disappeared. The Eastern (Greek and
Orthodox) and Western (Latin and Catholic[20]) halves of

---

[20] The word 'catholic' immediately suggests to our contemporary
minds the Roman Catholic denomination as against other confessions like Eastern Orthodoxy and Protestantism. However, in
looking back at this age we have to think 'pre-Reformation'.
Catholic means 'universal' and originally the description was used
for the sake of unity to distinguish the churches that held to mainstream doctrine and practice as opposed to its heretical variants.
Only after Constantine did the word 'catholic' come to hold real
political significance. After this came the East/West (Orthodox/
Catholic) split and of course a thousand years later came the
Reformation. It is worth noting two points here: (1) the Celtic
bishops almost certainly would have considered themselves to be
loyal to Catholicism right up to the Synod of Whitby and (2) when

the church had become divided and Europe was now completely overrun by the Teutonic hordes. Among a number of notable spiritual and political contributions he made to the life of the Catholic Church was a restoration of sung worship, hence Gregorian chants.

Significant as his achievements are, our interest in Gregory is limited here to his apostolic role with regard to the Roman church in England. His motivation for initiating the mission is told in a rather cheesy, apocryphal tale by one of his biographers. While still a monk in Rome, Gregory sees some attractive children in the slave market. He asks who they are, but when he is told that they are from a pagan people called the 'Angles' he replies, 'They're not Angles, they are Angels!'

However, it is highly probable that Gregory's motives in sending a mission to England were mixed. As we mentioned earlier, there was no love lost between the Celts and the Saxons[21] and the former seem to have made little attempt to evangelise the latter in the fifth and sixth centuries.[22] The severe brutality of the invasions and the consequent transformation of the British Isles clearly left deep wounds in the hearts and lives of the most pious

---

we speak of a Celtic/Roman split we are not suggesting that the heirs of the Roman 'spirit' can simply be equated with the modern Roman Catholic Church.

[21] To put it simply, by the time we reach 600, the majority of the Teutonic peoples in Great Britain are Saxons. The Angles were in the minority, but because they were considered a ruling tribe we speak of Anglo-Saxons, and 'Angleland' takes its name from them. Augustine began his mission in *Cantwara* (Kent), which was the land invaded and occupied by the Jutes.

[22] This reluctance was certainly true of the Welsh and other Western British Christians. As we saw in the last section, after the founding of Lindisfarne in the seventh century, significant evangelism took place among the Saxon nations.

Celtic saints. Many preferred to allow their peregrinations to take them to other Celtic shores, around England to mainland Europe or west to Iceland, Greenland and beyond.

So, from that perspective, it was clearly with something of a heart for the lost that Gregory sent Augustine and his church-planting team of forty monks to England. Yet Gregory also had some serious concerns about the Celtic church. He not only resented its attitude to the Anglo-Saxons; there were other issues. While technically subordinate to Rome, the Celtic church probably appeared as something quite wild and maverick to Gregory. For a start, to speak of 'the Celtic church' gives a false impression of structural unity. Without any outright rebellion (they probably did not perceive any problem with being Roman or Catholic at this time), the Irish and Welsh bishops thought and acted in a very independent way.

What's more, the Celts followed certain practices that owed more to the Orthodox tradition than to the Catholic tradition. These included the questions of the dating of Easter and the formula for baptism. Interestingly, one of the other classic issues of disagreement between Rome and the Celts was the style of tonsure (the bald patch created to show you were a monk). The Romans preferred the circular bald pate, whereas the Celts wanted to maintain continuity with the pre-Christian custom of the Druids, shaving off the hair from the front of their heads and letting the back grow long! This is another example of the Celts looking for connections with the culture, while the Romans wanted uniformity.

Perhaps Gregory was concerned with the detail or perhaps he was concerned with what these issues represented. No doubt he felt that a mission to the Anglo-

Saxons was a chance to bring the Celtic church into line. From the beginning, then, we must accept that whatever well was dug by the Gregorian mission it was impure, in the sense that it contained a mixture of motives.

Archbishop of Canterbury

In 596 Augustine, a Sicilian by birth, left Rome for England with forty other monks. Although they twice wanted to turn back, they finally arrived in Kent by Easter 597. Because the wife of King Ethelbert of Kent was a Catholic it was quite easy for Augustine to establish a foothold there.[23] Essex and East Anglia were then under Kent's control, so three out of the twelve Anglo-Saxon kingdoms soon became Catholic. Augustine set up a base in Canterbury and at the end of the year Gregory appointed him Archbishop of England.

It is difficult to measure the extent of Augustine's success in evangelising the Saxons. Some reports suggest that the rate of conversions was painfully slow, thanks to Augustine's rather unimaginative approach and the intense political and religious rivalry between the Saxon kingdoms. Meanwhile, Gregory claimed that 10,000 Anglo-Saxons had been baptised by July 598. Some historians, including Jakob Streit, have suggested that the only way these statistics can be squared is if Augustine was rebaptising Celtic Christians into the Roman church.[24] If this was the case we can see that the Roman missionaries were vigorously pursuing Gregory's dual agenda. They

---

[23] Although Ethelbert eventually accepted conversion, his personal church in Canterbury had both a Christian altar and an altar to Woden!

[24] Quoted in Marshall, *The Celtic Connection*, p. 27.

were evangelising the Saxons who remained heathens and re-converting to Catholicism those residents of England who had been evangelised by the Celts.

There were a great many contrasts between the Celtic and the Roman in terms of style. One example is in the area of evangelistic method. We have already referred to the dramatic and confrontational approach of the Celtic believers. In contrast, the Roman method – as demonstrated by Augustine and Wilfrid – eschewed all such Old Testament prophetic drama and was more fitting to an imperial background. Combining a mixture of step-by-step mildness, compulsion and material inducement, the Gregorian mission modified pagan temples to Christian use, translated the old festivals to Christian feasts and saw that converted chiefs compelled their people to receive baptism. However positive you try to be towards Augustine and his team, the Romans come across as far less attractive and genuinely spiritual than their Celtic counterparts.[25]

So, having suggested that the well dug by Augustine and his companions was far from pure, can we identify any strengths within the Roman stream? First, we should perhaps remember the words of the apostle Paul in Philippians 1:15–18:

> It is true that some preach Christ out of envy and rivalry, but others out of goodwill. The latter do so in love, knowing that I am put here for the defence of the gospel. The former

---

[25] Mayr-Harting (p. 70) has offered an explanation as to why this difference seems to be so pronounced. He notes that while Celtic hagiographers were monks setting down oral accounts which remembered these saints lovingly, Bede has few sources for the Roman missionaries because they considered the Latin concept of *gravitas* – calm dignity, restraint in words and actions and a lack of levity – as a primary virtue.

> preach Christ out of selfish ambition, not sincerely, suppos-
> ing that they can stir up trouble for me while I am in chains.
> But what does it matter? The important thing is that in every
> way, whether from false motives or true, Christ is preached.
> And because of this I rejoice.

God has a way of getting his will done through people,
even if they are imperfect. This is at the heart of the
gospel of grace. Where Christ was preached by the
Romans, we too should rejoice. There is surely little
doubt that Augustine did reach out to the Saxons.

Second, we should refer to the value of the Roman
emphasis on order and structure. This was very attractive
to the Saxon peoples. One of the criticisms that is perhaps
justifiably levelled against the Celts was that their evangelism often failed to leave structures in place for the pastoral
care, discipling and training of believers.[26] Although their
custom of discipling through a 'soul friend' was a
wonderful ideal that we value, perhaps its practice was not
universal.

With the Romans this was never the case. They were
always quick to baptise new believers and in consultation
with local kings and chiefs divide up the land into parishes
and dioceses. Some historians have argued that the
Saxons preferred the more rigid governing parochial
structure of the Roman church. Certainly it gave their
leaders more control over the population at large.

Augustine's Oak

Most historians mark the Synod of Whitby in 664 as the
time when the tide turned on Celtic Christianity.

---

[26] A notable exception to this is Patrick, but then he was trained in
Gaul, perhaps with some Roman influence.

However, it was an event prior to that which was perhaps more significant in setting the general atmosphere. This event truly marked the failure of the Celtic and the Roman streams to merge into one river.

After five years in England, Augustine decided that it was time to try to work things out with the Celtic bishops. At this time, although Iona was generally acknowledged as having a place of authority over the Celtic church, the Romans' contacts had been mainly with Christians in the west of Britain. Because of the bitter animosity between the Welsh and the Saxons, Augustine had struggled to communicate with the British bishops. Rather unsurprisingly, when he finally did so around 602 they were unwilling to travel to Canterbury.

Instead it was agreed that the parties should meet at a place recorded as 'Augustine's Oak' on the border of the Hwiccas (roughly equivalent to present Worcestershire) and Wessex. This site has traditionally been identified with Aust by the M4 Severn Bridge over the Bristol Channel. Others have argued that the spot was in Down Ampney, near Cricklade, on the land border of the Hwiccas and Wessex. It would have been considered safe because in Hwiccas lived a Saxon people who were allied with the Welsh against the West Saxons. Given the magnitude of its implications, it is worth recounting this incident in some detail.

According to Bede, Augustine's main purpose in this conference was to persuade the British bishops to keep Catholic peace with him. Additionally, he wanted their help in evangelising the heathen, for the Celts to keep Easter Sunday at the proper time according to the Roman tradition, and to follow many other practices of the Roman church. Of particular concern were differences in the rite of baptism and the issue of the clergy's style of tonsure, mentioned above. After a long dispute, the bishops were unwilling to follow Augustine and his companions and to give their assent, preferring their own traditions. Augustine is said to have brought the long and wearisome struggle to an end by saying: 'Let us pray God who makes men to be of one mind in his Father's house show us by heavenly signs which tradition is to be followed and by what paths we must hasten to enter his kingdom. Let some sick man be brought, and let the faith and practice of him by whose prayers he is healed be considered as in accordance with God's will and proper for us all to follow.'

All parties agreed reluctantly and a blind Englishman was brought forward. He was presented to the British bishops, but they could not heal him. Then Augustine prayed that God would restore sight to the blind man. At once the blind man's sight was restored and all acknowledged Augustine to be 'a true herald of the heavenly light'. Then the Britons are supposed to have confessed that they realised that it was the true way of righteousness which Augustine preached. However, they also said that they could not disown their former customs without the consent and approval of their own people.

Because a consultation process was requested by the British bishops it was obvious that a second conference should be held during which more bishops could attend. At the second conference in 603 we are told that seven British bishops and many learned men came, chiefly from a famous monastery called Bangor Iscoed, about twelve miles south of Chester. Even Bede accepts that the strength of the Welsh turnout indicated the importance of the issue raised and the willingness to negotiate.

Before the bishops set out for the conference, we are told that they first sought some guidance from a holy man who lived as a hermit among them. Should they abandon their own traditions for the preaching of Augustine? He advised them to follow Augustine if they were sure he was a man of God. Enquiring how they might know if he was such a man, the hermit answered, 'The Lord said, "Take my yoke upon you and learn from me, for I am gentle and humble in heart." [Mt 11:29] If this Augustine is meek and lowly of heart, we may well suppose that he bears the yoke of Christ himself and is offering it to you to bear; but if he is harsh and proud, it follows that he is not from God and we have no need to regard what he says.'

Still not satisfied with this they asked how they would know Augustine's heart. The hermit's solution was simple: 'Make sure that he and his followers arrive first at the meeting place and if on your approach he will rise to meet you then you will know that he is a servant of Christ and you will listen to him obediently. But if he despises you and is not willing to rise in your presence, even though you are the larger party, you should despise him in return.'

They did as the hermit had said and it happened that Augustine remained seated while they were coming in. When they saw this they became angry, having noted him as a proud man, and they argued against everything he said. Seeing he was getting nowhere Augustine tried to cut a deal. He agreed to abandon all his other requests if the Celts would yield to him on Easter, baptism and preaching the gospel to the English people. The bishops replied that they would do none of these things nor would they accept him as their archbishop. Now Augustine grew angry and, according to Bede, he uttered a terrible, threatening prophecy that if they refused to accept peace from their brothers in Christ, they would have to accept war from their enemies. If they would not preach the faith to the English nation, they would one day suffer the vengeance of death at the hands of these enemies. The conference ended in complete failure.

The story continues that this prophecy was fulfilled in a dreadful way some years later. On the eve of the Battle of Chester, the monks of Bangor Iscoed were praying for the victory of the Celtic warriors against their Saxon neighbours. By divination, a medium discovered that this was going on and told the Saxon king concerned. He therefore gave instructions for his army to attack the monastery before engaging the Welsh army. This they did, killing over a thousand monks in the process, after which they won the battle and further pushed back the Celts in that territory.

This whole story makes depressing reading for any Christian. The sins on both Augustine's side and on that of the Welsh bishops are multiple. For example, were not the Welsh bishops mature enough men to evaluate Augustine's heart without resort to such a childish sign? Does not Augustine's manner suggest that indeed he did view the Celtic bishops in an arrogant way? Was not some flexibility possible on either side? These examples pale into insignificance against the greater sin of Augustine's curse upon the Celts. Surely this event, rather than the confirmation of Roman authority over England at Whitby, was where the streams missed one another so badly.

Conclusion

In this chapter we have described three wells dug by people of very diverse backgrounds seeking to serve God in these islands. Exploring the work that they have done and honouring the best of that work has value indeed.

Prayerfully asking God to unblock the ancient wells as well as digging new wells of our own is also of great value. This story also presents us with another challenge: a suggestion of unfinished business that was left back there somewhere between the Severn and the Thames fourteen centuries ago.

We have made it quite clear that we relate most closely to the Celtic stream. As mentioned in the Introduction this does not mean that we are naively optimistic about the Celts. We have tried to be fair to the Roman stream without being deliberately polemical. As with any issue of conflict we might like to consider, the matter is not black and white. To draw a rigid line between Roman and Celt is just not feasible. Ninian was trained in Rome, Wilfrid was born at Lindisfarne, and so it goes on. Nonetheless, the events of 602–3 that came to be confirmed in 664 were of monumental importance to these islands. They resulted in the domination of the Roman stream and the eclipse of the Celtic stream, eventually capping that well.[27] There were still great leaders and missionaries sent throughout Europe after 664, but the church in these islands gradually became stagnant and generally lifeless compared to the days of the Celtic pioneers.

At the start of this chapter we wrote of the power of streams flowing together. The possibility of the Celtic and Roman wells working for the same goals offers an awesome prospect in hindsight. The strengths of the Eastern and Western expressions of church could both

---

[27] The decline of many Celtic communities was hastened by the ravaging invasions of the Vikings and Danes. This is an important fact in the course of events, and not one that we are seeking to ignore. However, at this point the Roman/Celtic divide appears to be the primary issue that needs addressing.

have been expressed in these islands. Order and energy, discipline and wandering, structure and freedom hand in hand would have been a <u>dynamic mix</u>. Instead we had a great divide. Not just an ecclesiastical divide but one that we believe deepened the chasm between the Celtic peoples and the English peoples in these islands. Fourteen hundred years later we still live with these divides and we will return to discuss them in the final chapter.

Eternity

3

A New Rhythm for a New Generation

As we look for the shape of the church of tomorrow, we predict that we shall find elements from the past rediscovered and reinterpreted for our creative dialogue with contemporary culture.

Taking the shape of the future

One thing is for certain: there will be both threads of continuity and elements of discontinuity about God's work in these days. This is a phenomenon we can observe in the Bible. For instance, in the relationship between the Old and the New Covenant. The Old Covenant concepts of sacrifice, the Temple and the priesthood all appear in the New Testament, but their appearance reflects both continuity and discontinuity in relationship to their form in the Old Covenant. The sacrifices, Temple and priesthood all find their climax, fulfilment and therefore an element of discontinuity in Christ. He was the perfect sacrifice (Heb 10:10), the fulfilment of the Temple (Jn 2:21) and is our great High Priest (Heb 3:1). At the same time the sacrifices, Temple and priesthood continue to be reflected in the people of God as they are in Christ, both individually and corporately (Rom 12:1–2; 1 Pet 2:9). This kind of paradox can also be observed from age to age and also across different continents simultaneously, as we examine the work of God and learn from it.

In history there are both common threads and startling differences between great moves of God. Currently the same observations could be made of the activity of God in Korea, China, South America, Eastern Europe, Canada, the United States and indeed the United Kingdom. Remarkable similarities, yet startling differences! God is bigger than any sacred cow, systematic theology, hermeneutical principle, denominational, non-denominational or new church distinctive!

Paradigm shifts

Moving into God's future always requires a paradigm shift. Historically the emerging generations have a better track record when it comes to successful transformation. This is why young people are always so prevalent in revival. From the previous generation only Joshua and Caleb made the successful shift from wilderness to Promised Land (Num 14:26–65). The apostle Peter needed a waking vision (Acts 10:9–48) and supernatural phenomena to change paradigms and include the Gentiles in God's plan. Even after that he still failed to express fully the inclusion of Gentiles alongside Jews and needed Paul's rebuke to keep him on the straight and narrow (Gal 2:11–14). Is your church movement (or indeed company or business) ready for a paradigm shift? If not, you risk becoming nostalgic rather than prophetic, and part of history rather than participants in the future.

Where do we go?

Obviously our primary source of inspiration will be Scripture itself. Many times Scripture will light our path, provide us with frameworks and interpret events ('this is that' – Acts 2:16–21). We also need to throw ourselves before God, asking for wisdom and revelation, because study alone will never form the whole picture.

At the same time history is a key for us. To engage with past church movements and see how they interpreted and incarnated biblical Christianity in their own time can provide both inspiration and instruction. Celtic Christianity is by no means the only movement that is worthy of our reflection, but in our opinion it holds some keys that are vitally relevant for these days. As we engage with the Celtic inheritance we believe we encounter a historical symbol that both encapsulates and illuminates much of God's activity in both the church and mainstream Western culture. We will experience both continuity and discontinuity and will probably have some of our paradigms challenged!

As we do this we need to engage with the future. God is not just at work in his church. He both raises up and lays low the nations and their rulers; he makes use of the times and seasons so it was 'at the right time' that Jesus came. This was the right time in salvation history, the right time in prophetic fulfilment, the right time for the spread of the gospel to much of the civilised world through the common Greek language and the efficient Roman road system.

KAIROS

Sea changes in history and culture

Recent history has been characterised by earth-shattering change. Walls have come down between East and West.

The 1960s' counter-cultural hope gave way to the 1970s' excess and punk revolution, followed by the 1980s' hedonism, boom and bust, leaving the 1990s' generation disillusioned with materialism and feeling largely disenfranchised from anything that purported to give an all-embracing explanation of reality.

This generation is disillusioned with politics and feels completely alienated from political parties. It is the generation of the single issue, which is ideally portrayed to us by the success of organisations like Greenpeace, as well as other environmental campaigns. Both in the US and the UK, political parties no longer stand on their traditional ground. They market the personality of their leader and revolve around a mass of single issues in any attempt to lure the rising generation. In this process many of the philosophical differences between the major political parties have evaporated.

Today there are few heroes. Those who do exist are the Bransons and Roddicks of this world who have challenged the institutions and broken traditional power bases in their success. For many, the 1990s represent the death of all dreams – the American dream, the dream of unlimited economic potential – and so the associated anti-heroes are people like Kurt Kobain, who took the way out by putting a gun to his head.

These events have coincided with a widespread rejection of absolutes and the old rationalistic ways of apprehending, perceiving and communicating reality. The good news is that there is a widespread openness to spirituality in this generation; the bad news is that it's an openness to any spirituality! The old apologetic that affirmed, 'The Bible is historically accurate,' and quoted evidence for the resurrection and proof of God's existence is far less effective these days. The general response is, 'So what?' What's true for you is not necessarily true for me! People long for experience and want to know how our experience as Christians can possibly be more fulfilling, more true, or indeed *the* truth.

These are the days of the global village. Communication, travel and technology have effectively shrunk the planet. Society has been fragmented. This is the generation born in one place, educated in another and working elsewhere. Their parents are probably divorced and maybe remarried. They have brothers and sisters, as well as stepbrothers and stepsisters, who may be of a different ethnic origin. Their grandparents are in a home somewhere. They have been alienated from the opposite sex by generations of sexism, pornography, broken relationships and a gender identity crisis. Rootless, homeless and denied community and intimacy, and alienated from the older generations, there is a gaping hole to be filled.

These are also days full of paradox. The days of the westernisation of culture. From Tokyo to London, Moscow to Cape Town, Singapore to Milan we can all endure the reassuring taste of McDonald's or be assaulted by MTV. Yet at the same time nationalism and tribalism are on the increase.

This is the computer generation. The days of a new medium, the Internet, the information super-highway. Everything is done at speed. It's the sound-bite culture, where image is more important than reality. Communication consists of a series of symbols and sound-bites (rather like this chapter!).

This is the air that this generation is breathing. A generation open to the experience of the supernatural, but who find it hard to handle absolutes and moral convictions. Reality is virtual, and music, art and fashion are both new yet 'retro'.

Some of these observations may be disturbing for some and may appear at first sight to be bad news for Christianity. Yet many non-Christian commentators have more faith for a spiritual awakening than some Christians! They look at where society and culture have come to and predict a turning to religion at grass-roots. We see this reflected, for example, through increased media interest. The authors' own church has had all five TV channels expressing interest in filming what God is doing among young people today. God himself has allowed the 'times to be right'. The culture is waiting for a Jesus movement if the church can respond to the opportunity by being both revived and made relevant.

Enter the Celtic Christian movement – as model, inspiration and vital symbol.

New yet retro

In facing this dynamic and volatile cultural context, the church has to contend with many major issues. To be faithful to Scripture we must both incarnate and proclaim the gospel relevantly within our culture, yet our culture is progressing so dynamically that even newer churches are becoming 'land locked'. Where do the points of continuity and discontinuity lie as our past history encounters our future destiny?

The heart and content of the gospel message are unchanging, yet the outward form and expression can vary wildly from culture to culture and generation to generation. Jesus' style of communication differed from Paul's, yet our view is that both proclaimed the same gospel. Paul's approach in Athens (Acts 17:16–33) was different from Stephen's (Acts 7:1–53), or indeed Peter's in Jerusalem (Acts 2:22–41). The differences between the Jewish and Gentile New Testament expressions of church are obvious. Throughout the world today there is a diversity of expression of biblical witness and through-out history various movements have expressed the same 'kingdom' genetic code within their unique phase of civil-isation and history.

To be effective today we must be both new (relevant to contemporary culture) and retro (expressing a truly bib-lical Christ-centred spirituality). Furthermore, it does us no harm to have our paradigms assaulted by the continu-ity and discontinuity we feel with other valid expressions of Christianity, both today and in history. We need to be open to criticism and willing to exercise discernment, bearing in mind we are just a part of God's worldwide church. Every aspect of our faith needs to be 'remixed' as we retain the original lyric and tune while mastering a new rhythm and form for this hour.

Some would say that this was the genius of the Celtic missions. They carried the very heartbeat of New Testament Christianity, channelled via the influence of the desert fathers, and were able to express and declare it in a way that captivated their contemporaries. Their approach broke into the depths of paganism and pre-cipitated a major spiritual and social transformation in a way that the early Roman approaches were unable to achieve. To receive Christ unfortunately involved becoming a civilised 'Roman' (the conflict of Acts 15:1–29 all over again), a recipe for problems. Yet the Celts found a spirituality that was both radically Jesus and definitively Celtic. Cahill describes eloquently the approach of Patrick, the Celtic saint in Ireland: 'Patrick found a way of swimming down to the depths of the Irish psyche and warming and transforming Irish imagination – making it more noble while keeping it Irish.'[1]

This is the challenge for every movement and every generation.

History – springboard or prison?

History and tradition together can become a dynamic springboard towards new and vibrant expressions of a Christianity that will turn the world upside down.

Sadly for many their history is their prison. Early inspiration by past heroes has given way to an imprisonment to one particular paradigm, tradition or label and we believe that the living God will be captive to none of these. We hear a cry from heaven saying, 'Too small!'

As Christians we relate to one another under labels like Protestant, Evangelical, charismatic, Pentecostal, Catholic, Reformed and Independent, with any combination of two or three or these forming a new classification. These make us feel safe. We can often include or exclude people entirely on the basis of their label. We don't have to be challenged by people outside our closed system. In the meantime, while we run around maintaining so called 'orthodoxy', people outside the church feel completely mystified and disenfranchised from any of these labels and are still lost without Christ! The sacred cows of the Reformation, evangelical awakening, charismatic or new church movements are of little relevance to either a sophisticated Western teenage night-clubber or indeed a rural Chinese community. What they need is the dynamic and powerful gospel of Jesus Christ in their language and culture,

---

[1] Thomas E. Cahill, *How the Irish Saved Civilisation*, p. 115.

as far as possible without our imperialistic or historical prejudices. Clearly we have a difficult task.

Wine and skins

We are not going to stumble towards the fulfilment of God's purposes in our generation without a major infusion of the Holy Spirit – a spiritual revival, awakening or whatever you would like to call it. Some are 'wine people' (Mk 2:18–22). They are preoccupied with seeking a new move of God and see the moving of his Spirit poured out as the panacea for all ills. Others are 'wineskin people'. They want to get the structures or their worldview right and believe that if they do so (according to their paradigm) the Lord will not be able to resist them and will turn up anyway!

The wine comes from heaven, yet its texture, expression and the eventual means by which it is received will be dictated by the skin. The skin can positively channel or seriously squander the wine (Mk 2:22). We believe we need to be holistic in our approach, taking into account as far as possible the whole of God's truth and the different aspects of his work, both within the church and within society. Clearly both the wine and skin are of great importance.

Rhythms for this generation

What are the key rhythms which will resonate in harmony with Scripture and the hunger of this generation? Well, we don't profess to have perceived them all, yet we do believe that our encounter with the Celtic Christian movement has helped us further perceive and understand some of these. If you would like a more lengthy encounter with historical study relating to the Celtic Christians, then see our Bibliography. Our emphasis here is to identify some keys throughout this book and to interpret them today. We hope you will find this thought-provoking, even if you disagree with our conclusions.

Community

Sociologists and church leaders alike are observing a common phenomenon: that of belonging before believing. Our society has become suspicious of words, marketing promises and media hype. People are attracted by relationships and belonging. A community or a tangible human grass-roots expression of faith can connect with their deep needs, some of which we identified earlier.

As a result, many people spend a long time in relationships, linked to community, growing closer to Jesus before finally making a wholehearted decision for Christ. People may even encounter God's power tangibly, feeling the conviction of the Holy Spirit long before choosing to commit themselves to Jesus via the grass-roots relational network of the Christian community.

The concept of community will be a key in this age. It was certainly at the heart of the Celtic Christian movement. Their mission was always followed by the creation of a monastery (church). These communities were a combination of retreat, commune, mission station, hotel, hospital, social action centre, school, university and arts centre. They were power houses within their local community, which drew large numbers of unbelievers who witnessed a living faith. They were vibrant sources of spiritual energy, hospitality, learning and cultural enlightenment. Columba called them 'colonies of heaven'. Some were in small cells; others were townships of 1,000 or more. The community at Meath, led by Finian, is reported to have numbered 3,000 at one stage.[2] By the time Brigid and Patrick had finished in Ireland there was barely a community that was not connected to a monastery.

Such was their influence that their leaders often had a prophetic role in 'king-making' among their tribes. Certainly saints like Columba cannot be boxed in as either a church pioneer, penitent, prophet or miracle-worker. His influence spread way beyond the realms of church and monastery, towards the shaping and influencing of the power bases in his world.

These communities struck a deep chord in tribal society where family kinship was strong. Seekers and learners came. Communities replaced pagan learning centres. Whole fraternities of Druid scholars were converted en masse and their colleges turned into monasteries with practically no dislocation.[3] Centres like Iona and Lindisfarne were established, and from these bases most of Scotland, northern England and parts of southern England received the gospel for the first time.

While there was no rigid or definitive Celtic church as such, there were common traits. The monasteries had a name which could be translated 'people'. They were human in nature, a living network. The lifestyle of the monks was often hard, strongly disciplined and far removed from the comfort zone of the twentieth century and as such can seem harsh and ascetic. Yet undergirding this lifestyle were a love and passion for God, a vibrant life and a creation-affirming spirituality that are a challenge and an inspiration.

---

[2] Michael Mitton, *Restoring the Woven Cord*, p. 49.
[3] Bradley, *The Celtic Way*, pp. 73–74.

Into the mix

When applied to our current scene these lessons are invaluable. As the church goes into the next millennium it will need to relate to the hunger and longing within humanity for community and relationships. Institutional, programmed and meeting-orientated churches will be less influential. Relational churches that are turned inside out, incarnating and proclaiming the gospel in their communities, will have impact.

Furthermore, our models need to be challenged. In the UK we are beset by the model of the local and parochial church. The Celtic expressions inspire us to a big model of church, more in keeping with the New Testament. A church is needed that is both big and small; one that transcends demography and geography, yet expresses itself firmly in both; one that has both unity and diversity and is concerned with all aspects of personal faith, corporate community and social transformation. That church needs to be so taken up with the gospel that it sees whole people groups converted. It will be so relevant to those people groups that its expression will emerge from within their culture, in their language, styles and flavours, yet still embodying the counter-cultural values of the gospel.

To achieve this breadth, church needs to be allowed to grow and emerge in differing cultures in a way that is sensitive to their identity. 'Tribes' (expressions of church) need to be established in youth culture, housing estates, the business realm and within different ethnic and language groups. These tribes need to be a living and meaningful part of God's 'nation', a heterogeneous, cross-cultural expression of God's community which embodies the reconciliation contained in the gospel between the old and young, rich and poor, male and women

female and different nationalities. Later in this b
shall look at some practical ways this could be f
explored.

Dynamic leadership

Within the Celtic communities leadership was often prac-
tised by an individual and exercised in an authoritarian
manner. These traits are less palatable to our culture
(although more acceptable in others) and do not sit well
with our views relating to team ministry. However, we
can learn from their recognition and release of gifted and
anointed leadership. Their leaders were not ensnared by
a mass of bureaucracy or red tape! It is also worth noting
that their bishops or apostolic figures tended not to be
figures of pomp and authority who reigned over territ-
ories or hierarchies. They were generally gutsy pioneers
who sometimes led communities and who at other times
submitted their lives to the local leadership (abbot or
abbess), being sent out for the work of evangelism, pioneering and establishing new monasteries. Even as a new
convert, it was obvious that Brigid was to become this
type of leader. This story portrays well her determination
and independence of spirit.

> Following her conversion, her father, an extremely wealthy
> man, was appalled to find his beautiful daughter giving away
> his stores to beggars. Quite out of control, he threw Brigid
> into the back of his chariot, screaming: 'It is neither out of
> kindness nor honour that I take you for a ride: I am going to
> sell you to the King of Leinster to grind his corn.' Arriving
> at the king's enclosure, the father 'unbuckled his sword,
> leaving it in the chariot beside Brigid, so that – out of respect
> – he could approach the king unarmed.' No sooner had the
> father gone off than a leper appeared, begging Brigid for her
> help. Since the only thing handy was her father's sword, she

gave it to him. Meanwhile, the father was making his offer to the king, who must have smelled something fishy, and insisted on meeting the girl before accepting. When king and father came out to the chariot, the father noticed immediately that his sword was missing and demanded to know where it was. When Brigid told him, 'he flew into a wild rage' and began to beat her.

'Stop,' cried the king, and called Brigid to him. 'Why do you steal your father's property and give it away?'

'If I had the power,' answered Brigid, 'I would steal all your royal wealth, and give it to Christ's brothers and sisters.'

The king quickly declined the father's kind offer because 'your daughter is too good for me'.[4]

Perhaps we may ask the question: Do our churches encourage and facilitate the development of a radical, pioneering type of leader? Or do we knock the stuffing out of radicals, consider them trouble-makers, or favour a type of leadership that is great at maintaining the status quo but is unlikely to possess the future?

Empowering people

The diversity of the Celtic communities, and their ability to embrace the involvement of all, appears impressive. In their communities men and women enjoyed working together. They had both married and celibate members. The ministry of the whole community appears to have been recognised, and there are examples of children being used dynamically to convey prophetic messages, and being valued as they did so.

The role of women also appears to be far more recognised than within the Roman church. Within the church significant female leaders like Hilda and Brigid are very evident. They both led communities and on occasions

---

4 Cahill, *How the Irish Saved Civilisation*, pp. 173–174.

Man and Woman

women

out an apostolic work. The release of a similar dynamic today would not only empower over half our work-force but would release new life, energy and relevance into the church. However, these dynamics would shift the power bases in virtually all denominations. Historically, the more institutional a church becomes the more male-dominated it appears. So change will not be easy. However, we believe that empowering women is both biblical and timely in the light of contemporary culture. As the powerless are empowered, the heart of God will be expressed.

People are less attracted by impersonal institutions. They want to feel involved and able to contribute. Our society has been broken by the oppression of women and alienation between the sexes. Communities that give value to people, releasing them to encounter God, recognising leadership on the basis of calling, gifting and anointing rather than on the basis of gender, will find themselves in a position to surprise and capture the imagination of society.

Developing people

Discipleship was at the heart of the Celtic church. Each person had a spiritual director, or soul friend, who was a spiritual advisor, confessor and counsellor. Brigid was quoted as saying, 'A person without a soul friend is like a body without a head.'[5] It was not uncommon for leaders to choose twelve disciples and invest in them. Finian apparently had Brendan, Ciaran and Columba among his twelve.

The story goes that Cuthbert was a sixteen-year-old

---

[5] Bradley, *The Celtic Way*, p. 73. Others believe it was one of Brigid's contemporaries, Comgall (see Appendix 1).

shepherd and saw angels shooting around the sky and praising God. On his way to the source he saw the soul of a holy man going into heaven. This corresponded with the death of Aidan. The monk Boisil saw Cuthbert coming and took him in and discipled him. A short time later they both caught the plague. Cuthbert was miraculously healed, but Boisil was not. During the last week of his life they studied the Gospel of John together. During this time Boisil poured his heart into the young disciple's life, prophesying in detail with regard to his future.

We need a church that will lay its very life down for the emerging generations. A church that will not vomit out its emerging radicals but endure with them, embrace them and encourage them. They will need to feel that they belong and as such can be trained, shaped and released to take us forward.

The rhythm for this generation will involve the remixing of the kind of discipleship Jesus lived with his disciples and the early church imitated. Relationships will be within the intimacy of community life. Out of friendship people will be taught how to encounter the living Christ for themselves and be introduced to the radical journey of faith and lifestyle which flows from serving Jesus. We don't believe this generation has rejected Jesus yet. We believe it is waiting to hear about him in its own language and to encounter him in its own culture.

In one sense this rhythm is not new. It's the rhythm of Jesus Christ our Creator and Redeemer.

4

Eating at the World's Table
(The gospel and culture)

As believers in Jesus we have encountered the one and only – the Christ, Creator and Saviour of humanity and all creation. There is only one God, one Saviour, one gospel and one good reason for living and loving. Our only response can be to stand in joyful gratitude and submission to his leadership in will and word. Faith in Jesus brings light into our darkness, direction and purpose to our aimlessness and resurrection to the dead areas of life. Our hope anchors us firmly. It enables us to face the often inexplicable pains and contradictions we see everywhere in the suffering and injustice of this world. Grace and sacrificial obedience enable us to be healed, cleansed and to escape from much of the corruption and destruction we see around us.

In response to the Holy Spirit, true disciples will have enough faith to remain pure, thankful and resolute in the purposes of God. By God's grace they will have enough compassion to be continually disturbed, impacted and motivated to care by the often harsh realities of life around them. Movements are needed that will reject the reality-numbing injections of individualism, materialism and the Christian sub-culture. At the same time they will avoid cynicism and disillusionment like they would a plate of CJD-infested steak!

If the church separates itself from the culture in an unbiblical (and unhelpful) way it will become increasingly irrelevant and unable to communicate. At the other extreme, if it is absorbed by the values, morality and cynicism of society, then it will have nothing left worth communicating in any case.

We have already identified some of the challenges presented by the dynamic changes in society. How should we as a church position ourselves with regard to the culture around us, with its mixtures of beauty and ugliness, death and life, riches and bankruptcy?

The Celts and culture

As we have seen, the Celtic Christians approached the culture around them positively. They engaged with it proactively and with imaginative creativity. They related to the culture around them because they were part of it. This made their mission incredibly effective. We have also noted some of the considerable contrasts between the Celtic and Roman approaches to culture, mission and church life. As is often the way, it is difficult to make a cut-and-dried case for their dichotomy. There was much overlap and perhaps it is a little naive to eulogise about the apparent Celtic ethos and approach over and above the Roman.

However, some of the characteristics which made the Celtic approaches more effective have much to teach us and we believe the Celtic/Roman tension carries some symbolic (or prophetic, depending on your preferred language!) lessons for the church today. Their tension creates a framework through which the Holy Spirit can speak afresh to us.

Indigenous

One of the greatest strengths of the Celtic Christian ✳
movement is that it was indigenous. Pioneers like
Columba and Aidan were not just the original Christian
apostles to these islands, they were truly our aboriginal
apostles. Their expressions of orthodox spirituality struck
a chord with the people in that they led them into the
light of the gospel in a way that enhanced their roots and
identity as a Celtic people.

One of the key debates in the New Testament was
whether the Gentile believers had to become Jewish pros-
elytes in order to be genuinely Christian. Passages like
Acts 15:1–35 describe these often vehement disagree-
ments. Was circumcision necessary for all? Was the observance of the Jewish law, including the Sabbath, necessary
for all if they were to be truly regarded as followers of
Christ?

The eventual conclusion appears to be that the Gentile
believers should abstain from sexual immorality and meat
sacrificed to idols (Acts 15:28–29). In effect, they were to
obey the moral requirements of discipleship and keep
themselves from any form of syncretism tainted with idol-
atrous practice. Furthermore, the Jewish believers were
free to adhere to many aspects of the Jewish law because
these things were part of their life and culture. However,
adherence to the law would not make them superior to
the Gentile believers, and neither would it save them –
only faith in Jesus Christ could do that. When Jewish and
Gentile believers (as well as the rich and the poor) came
together in one community, then the fun started (see
1 Corinthians 11 and Romans 14).

This position enabled the early church to become a
dynamic missions movement. It enabled Paul to talk in

terms of becoming 'all things to all men' for the sake of the gospel (1 Cor 9:19–23). It meant that very soon Jews, Gentiles, slaves, women and all sorts of outcasts and oppressed people became the foundation stones of this new movement of God's Spirit on earth.

However, core truths can easily be lost. The diversity and grass-roots nature of the early church was facilitated at least in part by the persecution in Jerusalem and the emergence of other key centres alongside it in places like Antioch, Ephesus and Corinth. By the time the gospel was being proclaimed in these islands simultaneously by both the Celtic and Roman missions, Christianity had become the state religion of the Roman Empire after the conversion of Emperor Constantine in 312.

Whereas before Constantine Christianity had been an indigenous, grass-roots organic movement, now it could become an instrument of state control and be used politically. This is a problem that has beset the church since that time and even events like the Reformation offered no definitive solution. As the Roman Empire declined, so the Roman church sought to establish its own empire of 'Christendom'. Rome was to become the mother church and it was time for these rebellious Celts to come into line!

Sadly the historical Roman approach to mission was not truly indigenous. Rather than becoming all things to all people the gospel package often included absorption into Roman culture and values. It involved becoming 'civilised'. As such their approach can be seen as imperial rather than incarnational at grass-roots in the true spirit of the early church.

The same challenges face us today. Too often our sorties into mission involve not just the bringing of the liberating and empowering gospel of Jesus Christ, but also the deification of Western culture and values. We don't just export the New Testament *kerygma*,[1] we also take with it our dress sense, our methods and our Western attitudes to church, culture, music and lifestyle. As a result, in many cases we have brought a message of liberation within a package of domination. Rather than releasing people into their God-given cultural identity, we actually enslave them to ours.

These problems exist not just as we engage in mission in other nations, but also as we lead people to Christ within our own culture. The gulf between so-called Christian culture and the mainstream has become immense. The language, setting and approach of much of church life in the West means that vast amounts of what we do can appear meaningless at grass-roots in our communities. Converts are expected not just to respond to Christ but to be 'civilised' in religious terms. Rather than existing for the benefits of its non-members, churches exist to maintain their status quo. Rather than meeting in the temple courts[2] where the people are, we insist that people come on our terms. Rather than going to them and growing from among them, we insist that they come to us, and in that process we lose the essential dynamism which the Christian faith demonstrates when it is truly in the market-place.

New Celts will be looking to see a new movement of indigenous Christianity: grass-roots movements in different aspects of youth culture, in different geographical

---

[1] The basic 'essential formulae' of the gospel as proclaimed by the New Testament church in the Book of Acts.

[2] See Acts 2:46. Church 'in the temple courts' is church located in the centre of everyday life and community activity. It is church 'without walls'.

locations and among different cultures and peoples. Movements that are truly apostolic, founded upon the New Testament *kerygma*, yet radically different in their cultural styles, approaches and flavours.

Mission-based rather than power-based

At their most inspiring, the Christian Celts displayed an approach to mission that was dynamic, flexible and inspirational. Monasteries trained and sent out teams to establish new communities. One historian records that Patrick's entourage consisted of his chaplain, his body-guard, a stone mason, a carpenter, the cook, a brewer and a lawyer![3]

 Their missions sometimes involved deals with tribal chiefs and the conversion of whole tribes en masse. However, the Celtic church was essentially a grass-roots movement. Their leaders were often pioneering vision-aries and despite many human failings, their goal appears to have been a devotion to Jesus Christ rather than the establishment of a Celtic church worldwide. Sadly, the Roman approach does not appear to be so dynamic. Despite some of their great leaders, their message carried with it the conviction that 'all roads lead to Rome'. This spirit is widespread in the church today and is displayed by the commonplace 'You do the Lord's work your way and we'll do it his' attitude which is usually closely supported by the vibe that 'you can't be kosher unless you join us'!

The Vikings' instinct was to pillage, the Romans' instinct was to control and dominate, and the Celts had the instinct to pioneer, move on and be flexible.

---

[3] Diana Leatham, *They Built on Rock*, (Glasgow: Celtic Art Society, 1948), pp. 76–77.

There is a lesson for us in this. Our society is being radically changed. Institutions and power bases are shifting. Information and power are being decentralised (for example, the Internet). Networking and relationships are the new language of growth and development. In the words of Phil Wall, 'The future belongs to the networkers.'

Vibrant networks rather than static power bases

In this environment the traditional cultural approaches to the implementation of unity are under threat. Trade Unions, Mothers Unions and Student Unions, as well as many other established types of corporate body, grew out of the social environment of the last century. Postmodern thinking has arisen from the onslaught of technology and changes in attitudes since the Second World War. The change of climate at grass-roots in turn means that these styles no longer captivate and engage. The need for unity and solidarity remains, but their expression within the current cultural environment needs to be changed if it is to captivate people.

Unity needs to be organic, dynamic, relational and, in the current environment, expressed through living networks and partnerships. It will be both demographic and geographic – a unity in diversity.[4] Of course there is much in the New Testament which provides a biblical and theological framework for the practical outworking of a unity-with-diversity approach. Paul's teaching on the body of

---

[4] Mission in the contemporary context will have to take note of both different geographical areas and also different cultural groups within those areas. Therefore organic unity will be the flowing together of Christians from different localities and also different people groups.

Christ, for example. However, this teaching needs to per-
meate the depths of our being as well as our approaches.
In the words of Rodney Kingstone, 'The day of the
streams is over; the day of the river has come.'

Therefore to engage with this generation and contemporary culture, churches are going to need to become less
hierarchical, patriarchal, institutionally inclined and rigid,
and more flexible, dynamic and charismatic in their
approach.

These factors have presented a considerable challenge
to us in the context of our own church. We realised after
thirteen years of growth and multiplication that our
growth could easily plateau. The challenge to continue as
a dynamic relationally based community has meant a
complete restructure and change into a more cell-based
model of church. Our leadership culture is being challenged by the need to avoid being orientated around
status and function and being increasingly separated from
the heart of the community at grass-roots. These challenges have changed our course and helped our journey
to take on a fresh impetus and urgency.

We have realised that if we are going to see genuine
expressions of church within different aspects of culture,
we are going to have to learn to express our oneness as a
church in different and creative ways. For example, this
creativity will involve the release and empowering of
young people to establish meaningful indigenous
Christian community in youth culture. We will explain
how we are attempting to work this out in practice in
Appendix 2.

On the larger canvas, as we look towards church-
planting and mission in other nations, we are holding the
tension between investing our own values and apostolic
foundations into other settings without establishing our

own imperialistic vision of Revelation Church in another country. Our aim must be to serve, empower, partner and catalyse indigenous networks. We must desire to work together in a way that speaks prophetically of our equality and unity in Christ while respecting the diversity and unique contributions which individual 'tribes' can make to the bigger picture.

The tribes and the nation

One prophetic model that we have used as an analogy is the tension between the tribes and a nation. In the Old Testament, Israel was one nation consisting of different tribes. Many of these tribes had different functions within the nation and also different characteristics. As Israel wandered around in the wilderness each tribe had specific positions and roles in both the setting up of the camp and the preparations to move on again. Furthermore, in Ezekiel 37, when a spiritual renewal or national revival is talked about, the recognition and establishing of the identity of the individual tribes and their coming together are very much central to that revival dynamic. From our perspective, we believe that in order for the whole church, either in its local or national expression, to come to fullness, first of all the tribes need to be established.

We need to establish expressions of church within every geographic, demographic and people group. In all nations there needs to be an established expression of the Christian community which is fully indigenous. It is as we go about establishing these different tribal expressions of church that we will be able to experience a more holistic expression of the whole nature of church – that is, the body of Christ local, national and international being 'joined and held together by every supporting ligament [as it] grows and builds itself up in love' (Eph 4:16).

This leads us towards an exploration of how we can have expressions of church, say in a local context, which express a greater diversity. Rather than enforcing a mono-chrome unity through the establishing of a predominant culture and attempting to shoehorn every aspect of the community into the Sunday meeting, we begin to move towards expressions of church that are based around community and relationships rather than meetings. These will actually encourage different and diverse expressions of community and cell life, and even different styles of meetings within the one church.

Within this there can be times of corporate expression; that is, the whole nation with all the tribes worshipping, being taught or giving together. Also, we can be free to have times that are unashamedly geared around the tribes. Even churches within communities that don't have a rich ethnic mix could benefit from this kind of approach. We believe it would help them to break into areas of both youth and working-class cultures that his-torically have been poorly represented in our churches. This model will really come into its own when in urban development areas (soon to be over 85 per cent of the world's population) where, in order to operate more broadly, we are going to have to look at more creative ways of expressing unity and diversity in the same context.

This also helps us in the wider sphere. There is nothing wrong with having tribal identities. Denominations, streams or 'non-denominational denominations' should be free to build their tribal expressions and to shape, dis-ciple and develop each other. Belonging and identity are to be treasured, and the ability to work closely together through meaningful resourcing is a valuable gift.

However, these tribal identities should not exist in a way that is counter-productive with regard to the aims and goals of the whole 'nation', that is the whole body of Christ nationally and internationally. The establishment of tribes is a key to the maturity, breadth and dynamic of the nation. On the other hand, self-interest, parochialism, nationalism, denominationalism or theological superiority will obstruct the progress of the gospel and the reaching of those who are lost without Christ.

We need to find new ways in which the whole nation of God can flow together in proactive and dynamic partnerships at grass-roots. For example, there are established initiatives and groupings like the Evangelical Alliance, Spring Harvest, Alpha and March for Jesus, as well as newer initiatives like the cell-church movement, Ged and Fusion. These are the kind of dynamic networking partnerships that are going to emerge across the body of Christ to address a wide range of issues from friendship evangelism through to justice and community. The tribes will flow together and the nation will find diverse expressions.

A positive view of culture

The Celtic Christians provide much inspiration and many challenges for us in our approach to culture. They were a genuinely orthodox mission movement with a strong sense of both the goodness and the fallenness of humanity and its need for redemption. Within this was a very helpful emphasis on creation. Perhaps they are a model for us as we seek to redress the imbalance of some evangelical approaches which have over-emphasised the theological themes of the Fall and redemption without giving due attention to the Lord as Creator.

These historical imbalances have often left the church with a negative view of creation, creativity and humanity,

and with a sacred/secular mentality which consigns them
to the private and personal areas of life rather than liberating them into every area of life and existence. On top of
this a weak theology relating to the stewardship of creation leaves us with no apologetic, lifestyle or spirituality
with which to confront the growing New Age neopagan-
based worldviews which are in the ascendance.

The earth is the Lord's (Ps 24:1)

Often in the church you encounter an inherent negative
vibe when it comes to the expression of the gospel, community or any form of creativity within culture. People
seem suspicious. You are left feeling that to express God's
biblical truth through arts or contemporary music is less
spiritual than preaching the word. Tradition has
enshrined both liturgy and preaching, and at times it has
subordinated and rejected other equally valid (and biblical) worship expressions.

The church always seems to be ten years behind the
development of art and creativity within the culture.
Trousers for women, long hair for men, earrings and nose
rings and other forms of fashion have been condemned
by Christians in different generations and ages, despite
the prevalence of earrings and nose rings in the Old
Testament (Prov 25:12). Time goes by, and perhaps a
woman in jeans is not such an unholy phenomenon after
all!

These kinds of issues betray an underlying attitude to
culture which we believe is fundamentally unbiblical.
Rather than displaying a worldview rooted in Judaeo-
Christianity, the church sometimes has a view of culture
and the physical realm which owes more to gnosticism
and the imposition of personal taste than Scripture.

Within the Jewish mind-set there was the constant under-girding that the earth is the Lord's and everything in it. Therefore, as they expressed their worship, fasted, feasted and reared their crops, everything was done within a God-framework – they were not secular activities. The Celtic Christians were the same. The *Carmina Gadelica* has prayers for milking, prayers for washing and prayers for fishing!

For the few, therefore, there was little room for a sacred/secular divide. There could be no such thing as secular music, any more than you could have secular farming! All of these expressions were outworked in a life-style and environment of worship to the Lord. It was this kind of mentality that gave birth to Paul's teaching in Romans 12 around the whole concept of worship being lifestyle.

All human creativity, ingenuity, spontaneity and capability ultimately came as a result of God's creation acts and are a reflection of his image. These gifts have great potential and are neutral in their essence. They can be used either for good or evil and will be an expression of all the extremes in our complicated world. In this vein we must understand that God's image in creation has been flawed through sin and rebellion. At times it is also demonised because of the inception and propagation of human philosophies as well as the invasion of elemental forces. Our encounter with culture will be creative, dynamic and redemptive, and may also at times involve a measure of exorcism!

However, the basic reality underlying all of these factors is that the earth is the Lord's. Our theology of creation means that we are free to engage with the activities of creativity and to be involved fully in culture. We do this knowing that the enemy and his philosophies are usurping God's right as Creator to have his will and word expressed dynamically in all of those spheres. As we go into the culture, we go with the full knowledge that there is no part of our humanity and creativity that has not been touched by the Fall. We continually need the redemptive work of Jesus to renew us in spirit, heart and mind, in order that we, in turn, can have a redemptive influence and begin to prophesy and communicate the heart of Jesus within the languages, idioms and paradigms of the respective indigenous groups that are around us.

The only truly secular thing is sin

We are continually concerned by the common use of the word 'secular' within the context of church life. An overview of Scripture demands that we emphasise that the only truly secular thing is sin itself. Worship is the whole of our lifestyle. Yet in the church we advance concepts like full-time ministry, secular jobs and Christian leadership, and so create an unnecessary dichotomy.

It seems to us that the whole teaching of Scripture requires that we view all we do as sacred and the whole of our lives as worship. Every human being who comes into a living relationship with Christ is called to be a missionary servant of Jesus where God has put them. Therefore vocation is not the privilege of the essential few who get called into church leadership or preaching. Actually, the sense of vocation and calling is something that God wants to release to all aspects of life, not just within the context of working in the church. After all, this is where most people spend only a very small percentage of their time compared to the wider spheres of society. Some will find vocation within their career; others will find it within different aspects of their serving lifestyle.

These perspectives will release the church from its
ghetto mentality and will give church leadership a more
healthy emphasis. The role of leaders is to prepare God's
people for works of service. These works should flow out
from the redeemed counter-cultural community into the
wider society in expressions of cultural transformation,
service and embodiment of the heart of God.

Living out this theology would empower and release
inactive believers. There are millions who sense that the
only way they can serve God is to sit there like good little
church members and hope they make it into small-group
leadership!

The sacred/secular divide means that we have no way
of honouring, praying for and sending out extremely significant people. These may be involved in major works for
God in employing hundreds of people, creating art and
music that influences the masses, as well as investing in
our caring professions and communities at grass-roots.

There are many members of our churches who have the
potential to influence far more people for the gospel than
so-called preachers. These people should be recognised in
their jobs and vocations. They should be prayed over,
anointed and sent out apostolically to influence and proclaim the kingdom within their spheres. If this occurred,
then we as church would not be pushed into the margins
of society but would be right at the core of it. Of course
the sacred/secular mentality exists not just within the
church framework, but also outside. The attitude among
some that their job or vocation is 'where it's at', and that
church is not worth bothering about, often comes from
a sense of rejection, but it also represents a reversal of the
problem. Their work becomes sacred, and church
becomes a 'secular' extra rather like golf club membership!

If we can move towards resolving these issues it will help us have a far more holistic approach to mission. Just as the Celtic mission teams employed a wide range of gifts, so the work of the apostolic and church-planting teams in these days may include business people who are church leaders, church leaders who are business people or indeed church leaders and business people together, with those gifted prophetically, creatively and artistically.

There was one setting in the Indian sub-continent which had an interesting church-planting policy. Wherever a new church was started, one of the people within the leadership team of that church would also start a business, providing employment and regeneration in the context of the community. This is just one example of how God wants to break down the sacred and secular mentality that often dogs so much of our church life and alienates so many grass-roots people from our expressions of church.

These issues are by no means new and have been debated for generations. However, that doesn't make them any less important!

Creativity

Addressing the sacred/secular divide will help us in our growth and maturity in areas like the expression of our worship. Typically, evangelical worship can be very one-dimensional, whether it is expressed within a more traditional setting or indeed within a charismatic new church situation. It often merely consists of a seemingly endless time of singing, followed by a long monologue and if you are lucky a response and prayer at the end! Within that framework there is often very little reading of Scripture, very little if any creative, artistic or symbolic expression and often little time to enable people to think and engage with God more deeply.

Increasingly, we are in a society that is becoming more open to the symbolic as a messenger. This has been called the sound-bite generation and people are genuinely more open to be engaged by the immensity of God's truths through a more creative and at times reflective and designed expression of worship.

As you engage with many of the aspects of Christian Celtic art – its symbolism, its music and its rich bardic tradition – you see that it was a movement where the people expressed their worship and their spirituality in a way that creatively reflected their culture.[5]

In the world but not of it

One of the challenges for us as a church is to make sure that we are in this world but not of it. At one level the biblical teaching is that God loves the world (Jn 3:16), yet at the same time there are the exhortations that we should not love the world nor anything in it (1 Jn 2:15–16). The New Testament word 'cosmos' or 'world' can mean any one of at least three things. First, 'world' can mean liter-ally the creation and the array of the planets; secondly, it can mean the people in the world; thirdly it can mean the fallen world system, full of sin and structured and organ-ised in opposition to God. It is this expression of the world that Satan is identified with as its Prince (Jn 12:31).

So, as church we are called to express ourselves in rela-tionship with the world around us. There are many ten-sions. The tensions of both flowing with the culture, being all things to all people, while at the same time

---

[5] For further reflections on creativity, see Chapter 6 and Appendix 2.

flowing against the culture and breaking the values we see around us that are often created by sin and selfishness. We believe that in our faithfulness to the biblical teaching of mission, we should be like the chameleon – a creature which changes colour in order to adapt to its background. However, this chameleon-type quality only reveals itself when we are living broadly within the cultural context. As soon as we are called to compromise the essential *kerygma* and values of our gospel, then our chameleon qualities vanish and we begin to show up as red on a green background!

As the church in the world our dominant posture is to be one of salt and light (Mt 5:13–15). Salt is a purifying and preserving compound, while light is something that illumines our paths and provides direction. As we engage in mission we are looking to place ourselves right in the middle of the culture around us, influencing, preserving and providing flavour. In these areas we will need to be creative. In certain cultures it may be appropriate, for instance, to have 'Christian schools' (not our preferred name for them as it implies a removal of the 'salt and light' from the world around them) because either there is no existing education framework, or existing schools are extremely antagonistic to the values of the gospel. In these environments we can, like the Celtic missionaries, provide education and a service to people at grass-roots just because they are people and thus show them something of God's life and love.

However, in certain settings the existence of Christian schools and universities, Christian companies and other expressions of a ghetto mentality can in actual fact be a hindrance to the proclamation of the gospel. We can create a Christian sub-culture which separates our emerging generations from mainstream culture. It cossets them and denies them the challenges of expressing their faith in the market-place as well as withholding from those who are lost the privilege of engaging with others who express the gospel. We hide ourselves away and leave the world to rot, which seems to be alien to both the spirit and lifestyle of Jesus.

Our identity as 'light' means that we need to place ourselves in the darkness in order that our light can shine more brightly. In our desire to be salt we must not lose our edge – the heart, content and proclamation of the good news of Jesus. However, if our salting involvement has given us credibility before we visibly begin to proclaim the gospel, then our words are more likely to be welcomed and received.

Our challenge is to be a movement for Jesus that will be clearly living out the reality that in one sense there are no such things as Christian music, art or writing (the list is endless!). There is just music, art and writing! Our worldview, spirituality and cleanliness of heart will dictate the nature and content of what we express more broadly in these spheres of culture. In every generation we will need both Christians who are musicians and musicians who are Christians! Some musicians will be playing their music with a pragmatic agenda of moving people closer to Jesus, ideally into a place where they decide for Christ at that moment. Others have a different calling. They are there to influence, to shape and to cause people to encounter God's creativity and to begin to ask questions which open them up to the gospel. They are there to raise the spiritual temperature and to influence more broadly. In this they are not ashamed of the gospel, but they are operating in a somewhat more subtle way.

Despite the hard work of many within the arts over the years, we believe that the evangelical church traditionally finds these kinds of missionaries harder to manage. 'Why don't you mention the cross and baptism in every song you write?' Such questions and the underlying worldview behind them have caused many artistic, creative, intelligent, called people of God to be alienated from church, much to our shame. Often through our unbiblical attitudes to culture we have alienated them, causing their disillusionment and obstructing the call of God on their lives.

May the Lord raise up a new generation of churches that will be able to reach, disciple and release these people. Our effectiveness in this age depends on it.

Incorporating culture

Having set this framework we can see that the concept of a Christian culture is both naive and misplaced. In the Book of Revelation people from every tribe and nation are present at the throne of the Lamb (Rev 5:9). The Lamb has cleansed and redeemed them, yet they retain their cultural identity. To deny people's culture is to ignore the heavenly vision. Furthermore, the presumption that our culture could ever be fully Christian seems to deny our own fallenness. It opens us to culture blindness and to the 'God is British', 'cleanliness is next to godliness' mentality which is close to syncretism (the mixing of our Christian beliefs and practices with those of other religions and philosophies, which results in compromise and the pollution of our gospel).

However, following Jesus as 'lambs among wolves' (Lk 10:3) has its dangers. Persecution and opposition are likely. If that comes from both the world system and from religious 'Pharisees' in the church, it is hard to take! Furthermore, there is the deceitfulness of sin itself and the snares of the world, our fallen humanity and the devil. As we go we will need to be strong in the grace of God and in wholehearted obedience to him, because if we lose our spiritual edge we have lost everything.

The Christian Celts engaged with art and culture seriously. They were brilliant missionaries, but this was probably unconscious. They related to the culture so well because they were part of it. They saw evil in creation and culture. However, they saw the gospel as a liberation and emancipation for culture rather than as a means of dominating and repressing it. The Philippian injunction to concentrate on whatsoever is pure and good (Phil 4:8) certainly applied to the Celtic approach to mission. They kept alive the native traditions and preserved poetry and folk song. Indeed, were it not for Celtic monks preserving and copying biblical manuscripts and recording the history of the pagan cultures around them, we would know very little of their heart and would have lost these valuable documents. The Celtic scholars studied classical authors, made jewellery and also spent much time copying and illuminating the Scriptures.

The Christian Celts not so much converted but reinterpreted culture and reinvested it with Christian meaning. They stressed the morality of God and had a love of nature. They looked to release the hunger for spiritual fulfilment within all human beings. They tended to fill out the spirituality of seeking people around them. Therefore the Celts' evangelism was naturally inclusive but not syncretistic. Outside of the Celtic church we can see this kind of missionary technique being used. Often when missionaries moved forward they would establish cathedrals on the sites of pagan temples. Harvest festivals were set up to celebrate the good in creation and God as Creator as an alternative to engaging in fertility rites.

Christmas and Easter are examples of the church looking to find a Christocentric focus to help tribes that had embraced Christ to celebrate and not be a bunch of miseries, while at the same time providing an evangelistic thrust into the culture around them.

However, this must be done with clarity and care. Historians have distinguished between the Celts' approach of confronting paganism and offering alternative celebrations with that of the Romans. Augustine, frustrated with the slowness of his evangelistic efforts, seems to have christianised the Saxon feasts of Yule and Easter as an inducement to the pagans to accept Christianity! Their hearts were not changed. Their festivals were not changed, but they were now Christian. This is one of the challenges we face with the re-evangelism of Britain.

Today we need to be thinking creatively in these ways. Hudson Taylor, widely acclaimed as the father of the modern missions movement, encountered all sorts of problems when he grew a pony tail. Such things were considered by traditionalists around him as 'not cricket'. Nevertheless, he saw that it was in keeping with the fashion among Chinese men and this was the way that he had to look if he was going to relate to them.

The incarnation of Jesus is a model of God himself operating in this way. Jesus was not just the Son of God; he revealed himself as a first-century Jew. As such he would have looked Jewish and behaved in a Jewish manner. This would have been his 'style'.

If we are going to relate effectively as a church, we will need to learn to 'remix' our gospel into forms which are relevant. So Willow Creek's model of seeker-sensitive meetings is of little use as a blueprint to copy literally within our own culture. It is mainly of use in that it helps us to see that culture-specific expressions of church can be very effective in reaching one particular people group.

Sensitive and relevant culturally

The Celtic approach to mission was clear about sin and hell, but positive about humanity. Generally speaking they lived alongside people and shared the good news. They were not there to culturally condition people. However, it is worth mentioning that the Celts exercised clear discernment. They seemed to be aware of when to resist and exorcise, and when to baptise and redeem.

Eating the fruit of the culture

This kind of positioning and flavour flows in accordance with the Jesus-centred New Testament mission dynamic. In Luke 10 you have the sending out of the seventy-two (vv. 1–20). Usually, in our interpretation of this passage, much is made of the sending out, their faith and on occasions the miraculous phenomena which flowed from New Testament mission. However, it is worth noting that wherever they were sent they were required to 'stay in that house, eating and drinking whatever they give you, for the worker deserves his wages' (Lk 10:7).

This verse carries the sense of simple dependency on the Lord Jesus as we go in his name. However, there is also the sense of eating whatever is set before you in terms of the culture. Martin Scott has shown that this verse has some wider ramifications. Wherever the early missionaries were sent out, they were commissioned by

Jesus to eat the fruit of the culture and be *in* the environment that was around them. Therefore, New Testament-style churches will be those that are able to position themselves in the culture and eat the fruit of that culture in terms of its artistic flavours and tastes, while embodying the inbreaking of God's kingdom across the board.

This is not a style of mission that involves the imposition of a mythical Christian culture which in reality does not exist. Christianity is not a culture-bound faith which requires the imposition of an inflexible culture in the same way as Islam or Judaism for instance. It involves God's kingdom breaking into existing cultures which themselves reflect God's creativity and his image as well as the fallenness of humanity.

Therefore, every culture needs a redemptive influence which comes through the breaking in of God's kingdom incarnationally in the establishment of Christian community. This Christian community both communicates a Jesus-centred worldview and brings his influence to bear through its lifestyle in the context of society.

If it is right to say that there is no such thing as a Christian culture, then the sooner we realise this and set about the work of salting, lighting and transforming – as well as proclaiming the good news – the better!

As we eat the fruit of the culture we will begin to identify some of the key missiological issues of our day. We will look later at Paul in Acts 17 interacting with pagan culture. As we engage with our society we become aware of the incredible grass-roots stirring towards caring acts, justice and rights. Globalism and the media have made people aware of human suffering. Therefore, taking up some of the major biblical themes of justice and rights, and centring them in on Christ, is a tremendous way of opening up this generation to the proclamation of the good news. As we do this we will be flowing along with the same gospel-motivated heart for justice that the Celtic saints displayed.

Patrick had a notorious temper, which flared dangerously when he sensed injustice. When the British King Coroticus raided Ireland, taking thousands of his converts as slaves, Patrick remembered his own slavery and petitioned British bishops to bring pressure to bear:

> Patricide, Fratricide! ravening wolves eating up the people of the Lord as it were bread! I beseech you earnestly, it is not right to pay court to such men or to take food and drink in their company, nor is it right to accept their alms, until they by doing strict penance with shedding of tears make amends before God and free the servants of God and the baptised handmaidens of Christ for whom he was crucified and died.

As Cahill observes: 'The greatness of Patrick is beyond dispute; the first human being in the history of the world to speak out unequivocally against slavery. Nor will any voice as strong as his be heard again until the seventeenth century.'[6]

Many contemporary campaigns for justice, fair trade and human rights, and the boycotting of unjust companies, can be seen as flowing from the same heart as this aboriginal apostle.

As we move in the culture, we interpret it Christocentrically for the means of proclaiming Jesus. The Celtic missionaries led the way for us in these areas. The traditional Celtic cross, with the circle of the sun pierced by the cross of redemption, is a traditional Christian symbol which communicates many different

---

6 Cahill, *How the Irish Saved Civilisation*, p. 114.

things. There are different accounts of what the Celts meant by this cross, but it seems to us to reflect that Jesus himself is the Lord of creation. Creation itself has been pierced by the cross of salvation and Jesus himself is supreme and authoritative over all the elemental spirits. The Celts took a common pagan symbol and reinterpreted it for the gospel.

Recently we heard with amusement that some Christian students had put an advertisement for a club night up in the window of their house. The heading was 'Pure Sex'! When asked by the people around them what they meant by this, they said that as Christians they were into a biblical understanding of sex and therefore they would only be happy with sex within the foundation and framework of marriage!

This caused both amusement and consternation, and opened up many conversations. After some dialogue, one of their non-Christian friends went to the poster and wrote under 'Pure Sex': 'Only within marriage'! In some ways this is a trivial example, but it illustrates how we can use contemporary logos and slogans, reinterpreting them in a way that enables us to engage them in the name of Jesus.

 As creation-orientated Christians it would often be helpful if we could learn to be defined by what we are for, rather than by what we are against. Traditionally speaking, Evangelicals are generally known for the things they want to ban or prevent. Rather than becoming known for what we are doing as a result of our beliefs, we are now known for what we believe, irrespective of what we are doing! This defensive positioning means that we are considered by some to be of little use and of not having a major part to play in society. As a result, in some people's eyes we have very little of worth to communicate. If people could see that our beliefs actually mean that we are acting proactively and positively in the culture on behalf of the whole of humanity, then this would open them to the proclamation of God's word in a new and vibrant way.

Justice

5

Towards a Post-Modern Mission Dynamic

There are four important points in the Book of Acts
which will help us to develop some of the thoughts
introduced in the last chapter. Although we will not be
able to give an exhaustive treatment to these verses,
each of these four passages provides us with paradigms
or frameworks for the development of church and
mission into the future. We believe they give us further
biblical data with which to understand some of the
dynamics we encounter within the early Celtic Christian
movement.

All nations – Acts 1:8

> 'But you will receive power when the Holy Spirit comes on
> you; and you will be my witnesses in Jerusalem, and in all
> Judea and Samaria, and to the ends of the earth.'

Right at the start of the Book of Acts Luke builds on all
that Jesus began to do and teach as he recorded it in his
Gospel. At the outset he is keen to establish the focus
which was to come upon the New Testament church
and to record how, after the coming of the Holy Spirit,
they continued spreading the message of Jesus through

111

the establishment of churches right across the civilised world.

In this verse Jesus outlines the clear priority and orientation for his people. It comes in the context of speculation over what Jesus is going to do after his resurrection and ascension. Jesus clearly states that now is not the time for endless eschatological speculation but to focus on the coming of the Holy Spirit, who will propel us as witnesses towards the ends of the earth.

The whole point of the coming of the Holy Spirit is to launch us outwards in order to complete and fulfil the commission of Jesus. This going to the ends of the earth is to be as 'witnesses'. The root of the Greek word 'witness' is that of 'martyr'. It carries the idea of a message embodied in sacrificial lifestyle. Therefore our destiny is not to sit there 'looking to the sky' but to concentrate and focus on the challenge of reaching every person in every age and every community, city and nation with biblical, incarnational and effective witness to the good news of Jesus.

Every church and movement needs to pulsate with this primary aim and purpose. Without it we will miss something that is fundamental to our identity and destiny in any age and within any generation.

Certainly the Celtic Christian missionaries had a dynamic sense of their calling to all nations. For them Abraham was a hero. The sense of journeying towards a place to which you have been called, but which in reality you know nothing about, seemed to stimulate their natural Celtic wandering instincts! They had a natural desire to pioneer. Such an emphasis will provoke and shake the very safety and often moribund nature of much of Western Christianity. We need to get out there to all nations.

All languages – Acts 2:5–7

> Now there were staying in Jerusalem God-fearing Jews from every nation under heaven. When they heard this sound, a crowd came together in bewilderment, because each one heard them speaking in his own language. Utterly amazed, they asked: 'Are not all these men who are speaking Galileans?'

There is much that could be said by way of providing a broad framework and understanding of the coming of the Holy Spirit that we see in Acts 2. This activity of God can be seen as part of the act of salvation begun at the cross. The death, resurrection and ascension of Jesus are completed by the coming of the Spirit. In this sense Pentecost is unrepeatable. It can also be seen as the equipping of the apostles, as well as the inauguration of a new era of the Spirit and the seal of the New Covenant. On top of this Pentecost is the first revival, and as you look through the rest of the New Testament and also church history you see that it is certainly not to be the last! Furthermore, Pentecost was a sign. When the Holy Spirit came, people spoke in other tongues and all of the dispersed Jews present heard the message in their own language.

At a practical level, the coming of the Holy Spirit reversed Babel and enabled the good news of Jesus to be communicated across the language barrier. Here we understand language as the means by which we disclose ourselves, express identity and identify relationally with one another. If we want to flow with the heart of Pentecost we will be looking to see that the gospel is expressed within all languages. This will heighten our desire to translate, encapsulate and incarnate the gospel to all generations, nationalities and cultures. If we fail to do this, ultimately we will end up as an irrelevance. This is not simply a matter of literal languages and cultures, but also about some of the sub-cultures that exist within individual nations.

Recently there was a radio programme which stated that much of black youth culture in New York which revolved around rap and hip-hop music had been completely infiltrated and dominated by 'the Nation of Islam'. The commentator said that while Christians were at home in bed behind closed doors with their burglar alarms on, representatives of the Nation of Islam were out at grass-roots on the streets communicating their message through rap music, their fashion and in a language that enfranchised and related to black people who often felt dominated, oppressed and without any racial identity.

We are incredibly saddened by this report and stunned at how a heretical sect within Islam can in many ways be a practical model of what we should be doing within some of the indigenous youth cultures that exist in the world's mega cities.

All peoples – Acts 10:9–48

About noon the following day as they were on their journey and approaching the city, Peter went up on the roof to pray. He became hungry and wanted something to eat, and while the meal was being prepared, he fell into a trance. He saw heaven opened and something like a large sheet being let down to earth by its four corners. It contained all kinds of four-footed animals, as well as reptiles of the earth and birds of the air. Then a voice told him, 'Get up, Peter. Kill and eat.'

'Surely not, Lord!' Peter replied. 'I have never eaten anything impure or unclean.'

The voice spoke to him a second time, 'Do not call anything impure that God has made clean.'

This happened three times, and immediately the sheet was taken back to heaven.

While Peter was wondering about the meaning of the vision, the men sent by Cornelius found out where Simon's house was and stopped at the gate. They called out, asking if Simon who was known as Peter was staying there.

While Peter was still thinking about the vision, the Spirit said to him, 'Simon, three men are looking for you. So get up and go downstairs. Do not hesitate to go with them, for I have sent them.'

Peter went down and said to the men, 'I'm the one you're looking for. Why have you come?'

The men replied, 'We have come from Cornelius the centurion. He is a righteous and God-fearing man, who is respected by all the Jewish people. A holy angel told him to have you come to his house so that he could hear what you have to say.' Then Peter invited the men into the house to be his guests.

The next day Peter started out with them, and some of the brothers from Joppa went along. The following day he arrived in Caesarea. Cornelius was expecting them and had called together his relatives and close friends. As Peter entered the house, Cornelius met him and fell at his feet in reverence. But Peter made him get up. 'Stand up,' he said, 'I am only a man myself.'

Talking with him, Peter went inside and found a large gathering of people. He said to them: 'You are well aware that it is against our law for a Jew to associate with a Gentile or visit him. But God has shown me that I should not call any man impure or unclean. So when I was sent for, I came without raising any objection. May I ask why you sent for me?'

Cornelius answered: 'Four days ago I was in my house praying at this hour, at three in the afternoon. Suddenly a man in shining clothes stood before me and said, "Cornelius, God has heard your prayer and remembered your gifts to the poor. Send to Joppa for Simon who is called Peter. He is a

guest in the home of Simon the tanner, who lives by the sea."
So I sent for you immediately, and it was good of you to
come. Now we are all here in the presence of God to listen
to everything the Lord has commanded you to tell us.'

Then Peter began to speak: 'I now realise how true it is that
God does not show favouritism but accepts men from every
nation who fear him and do what is right. You know the
message God sent to the people of Israel, telling the good
news of peace through Jesus Christ, who is Lord of all. You
know what has happened throughout Judea, beginning in
Galilee after the baptism that John preached – how God
anointed Jesus of Nazareth with the Holy Spirit and power,
and how he went around doing good and healing all who
were under the power of the devil, because God was with him.

'We are witnesses of everything he did in the country of
the Jews and in Jerusalem. They killed him by hanging him
on a tree, but God raised him from the dead on the third day
and caused him to be seen. He was not seen by all the people,
but by witnesses whom God had already chosen – by us who
ate and drank with him after he rose from the dead. He commanded us to preach to the people and to testify that he is
the one whom God appointed as judge of the living and the
dead. All the prophets testify about him that everyone who
believes in him receives forgiveness of sins through his name.'

While Peter was still speaking these words, the Holy Spirit
came on all who heard the message. The circumcised believers who had come with Peter were astonished that the gift of
the Holy Spirit had been poured out even on the Gentiles.
For they heard them speaking in tongues and praising God.

Then Peter said, 'Can anyone keep these people from
being baptised with water? They have received the Holy
Spirit just as we have.' So he ordered that they be baptised in
the name of Jesus Christ. Then they asked Peter to stay with
them for a few days.

Here we have the Holy Spirit breaking into Peter's mind-
set through a heavenly vision. At this stage in the develop-

ment of the New Testament church it had not yet dawned on them that actually Gentiles could receive the Holy Spirit and be accredited by God, and that church could be expressed and developed in their culture.

This concept was not just new to Peter but it was likely to generate a hostile reaction from him as it would seem to him to involve a compromise of his truly orthodox Jewish values. But as he responded to the vision and found himself among Gentiles, he saw that the Holy Spirit came upon them in their culture in exactly the same way as he had come upon the Jews previously. This caused a review of his practice and proved to be a turning point in the growth and development of the New Testament church, as eventually it opened the way for Paul's apostolic work and the growth of the Christian church among both Jewish and Gentile communities.

This passage is a significant challenge to us in our context. Today there are many 'new Gentiles'. Generally these are people who in their lifestyle, tastes and cultures do not fit into the framework that has become the dominant norm for Christianity. The Holy Spirit wants to come upon people within their own culture, meet them in that dynamic and see incarnational communities established which can then reach out indigenously.

When our mission does not operate on that basis, we see the vast haemorrhaging of young people from the church above the age of fourteen, and the huge gap of the whole generation between about eighteen and thirty-five. These disturbing facts show that we have been unable to establish church that both reflects the values of Jesus and is appropriately contextualised within the cultures of those generations.

We need to proclaim the message and establish community that is genuinely for all peoples. Something that does not smack of cultural imperialism, but enables an expression of true, credible Christian faith. Once people experience a taste of church which is in their language and culture, it inspires them to greater depths with God and empowers them in their spiritual growth.

When people engage with Jesus in this way and are beginning to be discipled and nurtured, they will be enabled to reach those closest to them. As they are established in Christ they will begin to be transformed. Then they will be able to have the issues of race, alienation and fragmentation dealt with as they gradually become integrated into the wider 'nation' dynamic of the body of Christ which crosses all cultures.

This approach will enable us to see dynamic expressions of church both within our communities and planted out from them. We will have churches expressing themselves in different people groups and will have room in our theology to see people movements emerge where the Holy Spirit seems to swoop through one demographic or geographic community. An example of this would be some of the events in the two-thirds world where whole tribes have come to Christ. Even in the West, movements like the Jesus Movement of the 1960s–70s show what can happen when the Holy Spirit invades a whole people group. We believe there is great potential for many such movements today. The planting of church within club/rave culture could be one example of this. Unlike other areas of youth culture, the club culture is a distinct people group. It has a coherent community expression and various shared areas of lifestyle, some of which are very antagonistic to the values of Jesus. However, the establishment of a counter-cultural Christian community within that culture could have a dynamic effect, both in terms of winning people to

Christ and influencing more broadly the values of that environment.

All beliefs – Acts 17:16–32

While Paul was waiting for them in Athens, he was greatly distressed to see that the city was full of idols. So he reasoned in the synagogue with the Jews and the God-fearing Greeks, as well as in the market-place day by day with those who happened to be there. A group of Epicurean and Stoic philosophers began to dispute with him. Some of them asked, 'What is this babbler trying to say?' Others remarked, 'He seems to be advocating foreign gods.' They said this because Paul was preaching the good news about Jesus and the resurrection. Then they took him and brought him to a meeting of the Areopagus, where they said to him, 'May we know what this new teaching is that you are presenting? You are bringing some strange ideas to our ears, and we want to know what they mean.' (All the Athenians and the foreigners who lived there spent their time doing nothing but talking about and listening to the latest ideas.)

Paul then stood up in the meeting of the Areopagus and said: 'Men of Athens! I see that in every way you are very religious. For as I walked around and looked carefully at your objects of worship, I even found an altar with this inscription: TO AN UNKNOWN GOD. Now what you worship as something unknown I am going to proclaim to you.

'The God who made the world and everything in it is the Lord of heaven and earth and does not live in temples built by hands. And he is not served by human hands, as if he needed anything, because he himself gives all men life and breath and everything else. From one man he made every nation of men, that they should inhabit the whole earth; and he determined the times set for them and the exact places where they should live. God did this so that men would seek him and perhaps reach out for him and find him, though he is not far from each one of us. "For in him we live and move and have our being." As some of your own poets have said, "We are his offspring."

'Therefore since we are God's offspring, we should not think that the divine being is like gold or silver or stone – an image made by man's design and skill. In the past God over-looked such ignorance, but now he commands all people everywhere to repent. For he has set a day when he will judge the world with justice by the man he has appointed. He has given proof of this to all men by raising him from the dead.'

When they heard about the resurrection of the dead, some of them sneered, but others said, 'We want to hear you again on this subject.'

We would like to look at this passage in a little more detail as we feel that it has so much to say in our present context. Paul's approach to the pagans in Athens will help us to develop a mission dynamic for post-modern culture.

Paul was attempting to communicate the good news of Jesus into a culture that had no broader knowledge of Christianity. They did not have the benefit of a Jewish backdrop and their inheritance would have reflected a gnostic or pagan view of reality. In many ways Paul's approach was mirrored by some of the Celtic mission-aries. Perhaps the challenges encountered by both Paul and the Celtic missionaries could be seen as similar to ours. We are not in a pre-Christian era, but many would say that we in the West are most definitely in a post-Christian era. This is very much influenced by many neo-pagan, or indeed fully pagan, values. As such we believe Acts 17 is a critical passage.

Paul went to them – v. 17

Paul's approach was to engage the Athenians where they were in their own market-places. This caused them to question and indeed react to him. Their initial response to him was that he was a babbler muttering beliefs that they had no way of engaging with. However, his approach was stimulating enough to them in that it precipitated the questions and opened the door for him to continue to communicate.

This principle of putting church among the people is enough in and of itself to precipitate a major reformation in much of Western Christianity. The way our churches are structured often revolves around calling people to us – calling people out of their normal and natural networks. If we are to reach this generation we must find ways of putting church where the people are. We need to be asking where the temple courts or the market-places of today are and then we need to put church in those places.

Such a framework and perspective is consistent with the model of Jesus' own mission. In Matthew 4 he is seen going to the people and gathering them to himself. We have already seen him sending out the seventy, and it was these disciples who had lived with Jesus over the three years of his ministry. They had indeed seen how Jesus approached the proclamation of his message and the building and discipling of a community.

After the Holy Spirit descended at Pentecost the disciples, now filled with the power of the Holy Spirit, continued to do the things they had previously seen Jesus doing. So Paul took the gospel into the territory of those he was wanting to reach. As churches today we need to find ways of taking the message of Jesus to all aspects of contemporary culture, and we need to be ready and able to use the relational networks in each community. We are not after scalps, but we are looking to engage with people through their natural networks. In John 1 we see this networking principle in operation, where Andrew, Peter,

Philip and Nathaniel all come through the one relational link with Jesus. As churches we need to express ourselves within existing networks – within groups that are perhaps campaigning, working for justice or serving at grass-roots. Rather than setting up our own Neighbourhood Watch, we need to get in alongside these existing groups and begin to network the networks for Jesus.

Paul approached them in their language – vv. 23–28

The apostle Paul was very much 'Paul of Tarsus'. As he had grown up he had been immersed in both Greek and Jewish culture. As a youngster he had been discipled sitting at the feet of the great Jewish rabbi Gamaliel. He had at the same time been educated in a city like Tarsus which embodied the confluence between Greek and Jewish worldviews. (And he was a Roman citizen into the bargain.) Therefore, after his encounter with God it was very natural for Paul initially to reach out to his Jewish roots and then from that begin to communicate the gospel beyond to the Greek culture he knew so well. As people come to Christ we need to be expecting them to be turned around and used to bring the gospel to their own culture.

In Revelation Church we have a young guy from New York City who, as a DJ, feels very much at home in the club culture. He is extremely principled and genuinely passionate about maintaining the holiness and distinctive-ness of his Christian faith. Yet at the same time it is natural to him to express his spirituality in a language, lifestyle and type of creativity that reflects club culture. As such he is brilliant at relating to people who have come from this background. Using their language will mean that, in certain contexts, it could be both theologically and lin-guistically correct to call Jesus 'wicked', sinners 'sad' and the Pharisees a bunch of 'plonkers'!

Healthy and biblical theology of culture enables us to approach people in their own language. As we do that we will notice Paul's approach was not to focus first on what was wrong in Athens. Often in church we are renowned for our knee-jerk condemnatory approaches. We start by condemning people, by 'putting them right'. This seems to be at variance with the approach of Jesus who, when confronted with the adulterous woman, was not afraid to identify the sin, but also treated her sensitively and beautifully in showing her his forgiveness.

In Acts 17 Paul addresses the spiritual hunger and natural inquisitiveness of the people in Athens. Rather than instantly rebuking them and condemning them for their idolatry (which the passage says Paul did find distressing), he approaches them by showing an interest in their statues, and therefore identifies with them. His approach was rather like that of one well-known missionary who, when in a Muslim culture, used to sit on the buses alongside many dozens of Muslims and tell them their own traditional Muslim stories, but with a slight twist in the end to reinterpret those stories from a Christocentric perspective.

Again, this is what Paul is doing, and it flows very much in line with the Celtic tendency to take some of the cultural motifs of the day and reinterpret them with a Christocentric edge in order to draw people closer to Christ by providing them with a cultural bridge. Paul's aim was first to identify with the people in Athens and out of that to provide a cultural bridge by reinterpreting their spiritual longings and showing Christ to be the fulfilment of all of those.

In this context Paul is keen to engage with their language and to talk in their terms. He is not beyond quoting some of their own pagan poets in order to engage them in dialogue and again present Christ to them. This shows us that the 'chameleon' approach which eats the fruit of the culture is essential if we are going to relate to people who in their lifestyle are a long way from any form of Christian understanding.

Twenty years ago people often had some idea of the Christian worldview – the teaching and personalities within Scripture, along with some knowledge of who Jesus was and what he did. Today this is often not the case. Therefore, to engage with them we have to engage with their existing paradigms in order to bring them to Christ and introduce them to him. It is no use taking our preconceived mission techniques and expecting these to work in today's culture because we will find ourselves talking a completely different language. The presentation, heart and dynamic of our message needs to show a little more identification and understanding of where people are coming from.

Paul reinterpreted their language

This is the area where we begin to encounter potential misunderstanding. In Matthew 11:18–22 we see that the Pharisees misunderstood Jesus' approach. His identification with people and the way he operated his ministry caused them to accuse him of being a wine-bibber – that is, a drunkard. Similarly as we identify with grass-roots culture we can be accused of all kinds of things. Where there are unbiblical perspectives within the body of Christ it is easy to be accused of being worldly simply because you have a trendy haircut, earring or happen to be playing worship music that owes more to rap or jungle than an old AOR (adult orientated rock) or folk music!

However, we need to gear our apologetic according to the people we are reaching. If we are reaching a very conservative culture musically, then our approach to music should be very conservative. If we are trying to reach nocturnal night-clubbers, then perhaps our discipleship models need to be both nocturnal and also based around club music. It's horses for courses – all things to all people!

In this respect it is very interesting to contrast Stephen's apologetic and approach in Acts 7 and Paul's in Acts 17. Stephen's is very much Jewish-centred. He quotes heavily from the Old Testament and Jewish history. This is because he is relating to Jewish people who will be able to understand and be challenged by the nature of his message, because they can engage with all of those aspects of their history.

Paul, on the other hand, completely ignored the Old Testament when addressing the Athenians. In fact in this presentation of the gospel he does not quote Scripture at all. Following from this it would be completely consistent with Scripture to say that it is unbiblical to preach from the Bible every time you are involved in evangelism. Now there's something worth thinking about!

Paul started where they were at, in their language, using their concepts and ideas. Today in our communication of the gospel, particularly in areas of youth culture, we need to be looking at idioms like rap as potentially providing a model for street prophecy and proclamation. We need to be looking at issues such as symbolism, creativity, the use of fashion, image and media in order to make the content of the gospel accessible to people.

Making the unknown known – v. 23

As Paul begins to move on in his communication in Athens, he refocuses people's point of hunger rather than paternalistically correcting them or judging them. We

need to realise that in order to captivate this generation
we are going to need to be a little more subtle in the way
we present our message. In the past an emphasis on
things we now see as arrogant, like certainty and dogma-
tism, were more acceptable, even trendy. However, in the
current environment these qualities turn people off the
message before they even hear what it is. We happily
accept that our Christian faith involves plenty of wholesome absolutes and if we are going to communicate these
to people perhaps our approach needs to be 'non-
dogmatically dogmatic! That is, while being secure in
God's truth, we communicate it in a sensitive way, engaging in dialogue, both presenting and provoking questions, rather than preaching a monologue full of absolute
propositions.

As we take this approach we are able to begin to correct
people's error by refocusing them. This is very much
Paul's approach in verse 24. Paul initially uses the term
'living, moving and having our being', which could be
seen as a kind of pagan, New-Age-type statement. He
catches their attention by using this language and then
reinterprets it Christocentrically in terms of God as
Creator. Once he has done this he then moves into a bold
proclamation relating to Jesus and the resurrection.

Some commentators dismiss this passage, noting that
verse 34 indicates that only a few people became followers of Jesus through Paul's approach there. However, we
believe the approach Paul employs here is effective, fully
consistent with Jesus' approach in the Gospels and part of
the unfolding work of God's Spirit and the development
of the New Testament church into the future. We believe
this is the same type of approach which inspired the Celtic
missionaries to be so dynamically effective in their age and
we perceive there are similar lessons for us to learn today.

As we encounter the power of God's Spirit in this time, let us move forward in a way that is consistent with missiological practice in the New Testament. People deserve to experience church in their language and culture. Raising these issues will certainly not be easy for us in these days. It will involve much change, experimentation and a good deal of criticism from some of our more religious brothers and sisters. However, if we are to reach the 91 per cent of people who are no longer attending church in our own nation and thus avoid extinction, we need both to receive God's dynamic power and to operate in more radical ways.

6

Spirituality 1 – Exploring New Horizons

One of the most important issues for the church to address in these days is the issue of spirituality. There has never been a time, certainly within our era, when the issue of spirituality has been so heavily on the agenda within our society. In almost every sphere – religion, health, lifestyle, family or business training – spirituality is recognised as an essential ingredient within human nature and identity. As such, there is a phenomenal opportunity for us to introduce people to the Lord Jesus Christ who is both the summit and summation of all true spirituality and holistic lifestyle.

However, these opportunities coincide with a crisis of spirituality within much of Western Christianity. Liberalism, with its death-wish, has emptied so many churches. Furthermore, evangelicalism, and the Pentecostal and charismatic movements, as well as other influential strands within the church, are all struggling to express a fully biblical and Christian spirituality which engages the diverse needs and aching hunger of these generations.

Our initial encounter with the Celtic Christian movement came out of a deep hunger and desire to experience more of God and to find a breadth of spirituality that resonated with our own journey in Christ to this point. It provided further depth, breadth and inspiration to help us plot a path onwards, both personally and in our corporate life as a Christian community. Around us in the church we continued to encounter a disturbing slavery to modernity and rationalism, coupled with an inherent dualism which tended to relegate the Christian faith either to the private and personal or to the Sunday meeting. Furthermore, the absence of symbolism and expressions of rootedness in the context of worship seemed to reflect a kind of sell-out to the concept of progress: 'We have the latest revelation and this is better than anything that has gone before!'

In our view, this 'progress' has often involved a reinventing of the wheel and an establishment of a type of spirituality which, while at times vibrant, occasionally lacks depth. It could so easily be enriched and informed through an encounter with past movements of God which have much to impart to us.

Deep down in our churches there is a tremendous aching for spirituality. We believe that within the early Celtic Christian movement there are many keys and answers. If we can pursue these with openness and humility, we not only will come into a richer experience of the living Christ, but we will also imbibe a broader expression of spirituality that will engage more dynamically with the felt needs of society.

God breaking in (the now event)

Much of our spirituality within charismatic and evangelical traditions revolves around 'God breaking in' and acting at that moment in an individual's life, be it in salvation, forgiveness or healing. People are encouraged into a place where they encounter Jesus for the first time and give their lives to him. On an ongoing basis, in the context of their Christian lives, people are encouraged to respond in areas of repentance, faith, healing and in other ways which involve a 'now' encounter with the living God. All this is good. People of all ages need to be faced with the challenges of the gospel and given the opportunity to experience God's power and truth for themselves. People who are not believers are often genuinely open to experience the power of God at work. As such many of the evidences of God's Spirit on the move within charismatic expressions of church are both vitally important and very much part of God's heart and plan.

However, if this becomes a one-dimensional approach we can end up expressing a spirituality which is meetings-based and revolves around an experience of God intervening at crisis points on a regular basis. Consequently, people's spiritual lives can be mapped from one 'mugging experience' to another, or from one 'response' to the next. They no longer know how to fuse what they are learning and experiencing with Jesus in an ongoing way with their lifestyle. Their experience of a living God in meetings does not translate into their everyday Monday-to-Friday experience, filling it with increasing validity and purpose.

The lifestyle encounter

Following on from 'God breaking in now' we believe that the other key aspect of our spirituality we need to affirm is the lifestyle encounter. Encountering God powerfully and experientially is mind-blowing, but this really needs to be integrated into an ongoing relational dynamic. Evangelicalism and charismatic expressions of spirituality can be extremely individualistic and one-dimensional. Therefore, we believe that in this generation we are looking for a lifestyle to wrap around our encounter with God that engages creativity and community, while encouraging us towards calling and vocation, with an increasing awareness of the creation around us.

Human beings are asking questions about their identity. These days people are not looking to a disengaged philosophical system for answers. They are looking to the creation around and beginning to see the interconnectedness between humanity and creation.

This is where, as Christians, we need to have a clear and biblical theology of creation which recognises the role and connection of humanity with the rest of the created realm. People feel alienated from creation. They are now suspicious of the philosophy of progress and see that in many cases this has destroyed the environment, causing disharmony and alienation. In the past creation has been seen as something wild that needs to be domesticated – something that can be exploited and owned. Human selfishness will inevitably lead us in this direction. However, as Christians we need to be modelling a spirituality that has a greater handle on some of these issues. The book *Whose Earth?*[1] is an attempt to reflect on some of these challenges.

A Holy Spirit movement

The Celtic Christians were a Holy Spirit movement and as such they are deeply challenging to our spirituality as Christians. As we observe them in their earthy and often dynamic encounters with the living God, we cannot fail

---

[1] Chris Seaton, *Whose Earth?* (Crossway Books, 1992).

to be challenged. We believe some of these challenges will prepare us to face the issues confronting us in the wider areas of society.

One of these issues revolves around the clash between the church, which has become increasingly rationalistic and often seems to lack a vibrant and powerful spirituality, and a post-modern society, with all its experience of mysticism, occultic power and active spirituality.

As you read of the Christian Celts, it is not long before you realise that right at the heart of their spirituality was a power encounter with the living God. The evangelism of people like Columba often led to a powerful clash between the living God and the demonic and pagan expressions of spirituality around them. The following extracts describe two encounters by Columba with the Druid Broichan and portray a familiar scenario:

> About the same time, the venerable man asked the druid Broichan, who had an Irish woman as his slave, to pity her humanity and release her. When Broichan resisted most stubbornly and continued to keep her, the saint addressed him as follows: 'Know this, Broichan, know this: if you refuse to release this foreign captive for me before I return from this province, you will at once die.' He said this in the presence of King Brude, and then left the royal house and came to the River Nes. And picking up a white stone from this river, he said to his companions, 'Mark this white stone: through this the Lord will bring about many cures of the sick among this heathen people.' And after speaking these words he at once added, 'Now has Broichan suffered a mighty blow; for an angel sent from heaven has struck him grievously, shattered into many fragments the glass cup from which he was drinking, and left him gasping for breath and close to death. Here let us wait a while for two messengers from the king, sent to us in haste to ask our immediate help for the dying Broichan. In his terrible plight, Broichan is now ready to release the slave girl.'

While the saint was still speaking these words, behold, as he had foretold, two horsemen arrived sent by the king; and they described everything that had befallen Broichan in the king's fortress, just as the saint had prophesied, regarding the breaking of the cup, the seizure of the druid, and his readiness to release the slave girl. And they added this: 'The king and his household have sent us to you to ask your help for his foster-father Broichan, who is close to death.'

On hearing these words of the emissaries, the saint sent two of his company to the king with the stone blessed by him, saying, 'If Broichan first promises to free the slave girl, then let this little stone be dipped in water and so let him drink of it, and at once he will recover his health. But if he refuses and opposes the slave girl's release, he will immediately die.'

The two messengers, in obedience to the word of the saint, came to the king's court and reported to the king the venerable man's words. When these were made known to the king and his foster-father Broichan, they were most alarmed. And in the same hour the slave girl was freed and entrusted to the holy man's emissaries, and the stone was dipped in water; and in miraculous defiance of nature it floated on the water like an apple or a nut, and the holy man's blessing could not be submerged. Broichan, after he had drunk of the floating stone, at once returned from the brink of death and recovered full health of body.

This miraculous stone was afterwards preserved among the king's treasures and brought about by the Lord's mercy the cure of many sicknesses among the people, after it was dipped in water and floated in the same manner. Strange to tell, when it was sought by those sick people whose life had reached its close, the same stone could not be found. For example, a search was made for it on the day of King Brude's death, but it could not be found in the place where it had previously been kept.[2]

---

[2] John Marsden, *The Illustrated Life of Columba*, pp. 159–160.

One day after the events related above, Broichan said to the holy man, 'Tell me, Columba, when do you propose to set sail?' The saint said, 'We propose to start our voyage in two days' time, if God wills and we yet live.' But Broichan replied, 'You will not be able, for I have the power to create an adverse wind against you and to raise up a dark pall of mist.' The saint said, 'God's omnipotence rules over all things, and in His name and by His guidance all our movements are directed.' To be brief, the saint, accompanied by a large crowd, came to the long lake of the River Nes on that day, just as he had intended; while the druids began to rejoice as they saw a great mist and a storm raised up, with an adverse wind.

It is not surprising that happenings of this kind can sometimes, when God permits, be brought about by the art of demons, so that even the winds and waves are roused to fury. For in just the same way, when the holy Bishop Germanus was once sailing from a bay of Gaul to Britain for the salvation of souls, legions of demons confronted him far out at sea and stirred up menacing storms, hiding the sky and the daylight with a dark pall of mist. But at the prayer of Saint Germanus, and more swiftly than words, all became calm and still, and the mist was dispersed.

Our Columba, therefore, seeing the elements being roused to fury against him, invoked Christ the Lord; and boarding the boat, more resolute than the hesitant crew, he ordered the sail to be hoist against the wind. At this, with the whole crowd looking on, the ship sailed against the adverse wind with astonishing speed. And after a short time the adverse winds, to the amazement of everyone, were turned round so as to prosper the voyage. And thus for the whole of that day a gentle and favourable breeze continued to blow, and the blessed man's boat was driven on to its intended harbour.

Let the reader, therefore, reflect on the greatness and character of this venerable man, in whom Almighty God, by the working of these miraculous powers recorded

here, made manifest His glorious name before a heathen
people.[3]

The Celts' evangelism was often within the context of the
miraculous. Power, holiness and humility were a hallmark
of their proclamation of the good news. At times there
were incredible demonstrations of God's power breaking
out. As we mentioned in the Introduction, many commentators over the years have attempted to 'demythologise' the Celts and extract the miraculous in a similar way
to how they have sought to demythologise the New
Testament. We believe that if we attempt to rationalise
the miraculous aspect of Celtic spirituality we will be
eradicating an important part of their identity. However,
we need to recognise that their writings flowed out of
their own culture. They loved a story, and often its full
meaning was brought out by the embellishment of the
account.

One could ask the same question with regard to some
of Jesus' own stories. For example, with regard to the
parable of the Good Samaritan. Is it really important
whether there was literally a good Samaritan or a literal
inn on that road, or whether the event actually occurred?
Or, within the parabolic style of communication, is the
message of the parable most important in Jesus' mind?
We think the Christian Celts would have had no problem
in engaging with that kind of thinking.

In that vein the stories of Columba confronting the
Loch Ness monster (which takes one look at Columba's
upraised arm and makes a quick exit for the loch!) can be
enjoyed, celebrated and perhaps learned from, but in the
end we are not sure how seriously we should take their
historicity.

---

[3] John Marsden, *The Illustrated Life of Columba*, pp. 160–161.

However, within the Celts' story-telling and culture you can see that their everyday experience was permeated with both genuine and historical encounters with the supernatural power of God. Columba is recorded as confronting magicians over dead bodies and contaminated wells. Rather like Elijah and the prophets of Baal the challenge was issued – whoever's God is real will raise the dead bodies and cleanse the wells! There are numerous wonderful stories of such miracles resulting in the conversion of many to Christ and the spread of the gospel. The Celtic Christians had a confidence in God's inbreaking power which facilitated this type of phenomenon on a regular basis.

We can observe the same things happening in many parts of the two-thirds world today. The experience of the miraculous in places like China, Africa and South America seems to be far beyond that which we experience within the so-called advanced and civilised world. We have allowed our minds and hearts to be darkened by the cynicism of our history and are being robbed in these areas. The Celtic Christian movement offers a reminder and now calls us to account.

Encountering the enemy

When the Celtic missionaries went about the work of proclaiming the good news of the kingdom they appear to have had a variety of approaches. In some settings Celtic missionaries would boldly cut down 'occultic trees', thus confronting the spirits behind them. At other times the proclamation of the gospel would involve the laying to waste of pagan shrines or temples and their replacement with churches or monasteries. Both the mission work of early inspirational people like Martin of Tours, and the subsequent prolific activities of people like Columbanus in France, Switzerland and northern Italy, showed these characteristics. Cahill describes the achievements of Columbanus:

> At his death in 615 he left behind a considerable body of work – letters and sermons, notable for their playful imitation of such classical authors as Sappho, Virgil, Ovid, Juvenas, Martial and even Ausonius; instructions for the brethren; poems, lyrics – and the even larger legacy of his continental monasteries – we cannot be sure how many were founded in his lifetime and after his death. But the number cannot be less than sixty and maybe more than a hundred. He had been on the continent for just 25 years.[4]

If we are to move out of the Christian ghetto and place Christianity in the market-place, spiritual warfare is inevitable. If we do not go in with a sense of God's power and an understanding of the supernatural realm we are going to be compromised, broken and defeated before we have even arrived.

Our spiritual warfare will need to consist of the proclamation of the good news and the inbreaking of God's power through prayer. It must loosen the holds that the devil and his minions have on so many areas of our society and culture, in order that we can go on through acts of care, creativity and action and 'occupy the land' that has been cleared.

Proclamation in and of itself will not solve the problem. Without action and the appropriate prayer, we will not break through. Similarly action, creativity and other social acts in and of themselves are not going to see the break-

---

[4] Cahill, *How the Irish Saved Civilisation*. Here we see that spiritual warfare involves not just expelling the enemy, but filling the resulting vacuum with the positives of God's kingdom.

through. If they are not covered in prayer and accompanied by a proclamation of the good news, we will be lost. Furthermore, the beating of our breasts in prayer and spiritual warfare without the proclamation of the good news and the taking of territory through an engagement with the culture is also a vacuous and vain activity. We need to see all three of these aspects together if we are going to be truly effective – proclamation, prayer and action.

As such, the Celtic monasteries appeared, perhaps unintentionally, to display this 'holistic' approach. There was a supernatural God breaking in, yet at the same time there was the proclamation of the good news which was supported through the social acts of the community in feeding the poor, teaching people to read and write, and other areas of action and care.

The warrior attitude

Many of the Celtic leaders were converted warriors and fighters. In fact the environment in which the Celtic church arose was very violent, full of suffering and often extremely barren. The Saxon and later Viking invasions meant warfare was an unwelcome but familiar part of their lives. Merely to exist in those days required a sense of resilience and battling – almost a warrior attitude. When the Celts came to Christ these characteristics informed and influenced their spirituality. We believe that today, through the example of many of these Celtic missionaries, God is restoring the warrior to the church. This is not an arrogant and insensitive attitude, but it is an attitude that is full of passion, energy, fire and battle to see God's kingdom revealed. This generation has a phenomenal heart for justice, for the poor and the oppressed. Its

heart cry is an echo of the heart of God. We believe that
God wants to restore an aggressive attitude to this
generation so that with passion, activity and great power
we can be proclaiming, 'Your kingdom come, your will be
done in earth as it is in heaven.'

It is interesting to note that in many cases this warrior
attitude was coupled with a genuine humility. While there
were challenges to pagan priests which brought about
great victory, the Celtic Christians were reluctant to
engage in power plays with other Christians. Remember
the confrontation of the Welsh bishops with Augustine at
Aust. The Welsh were reluctant to heal the blind man and
Bede says they could not do so. We believe that the
natural instinct of the Celts did not enable them to take
part wholeheartedly in these sorts of activities. It was
against their philosophy to channel the grace of God in a
way that enabled them to gain advantage and position
above other brothers and sisters.

This is a great challenge to us today where it appears
that the experience of the supernatural within Christianity
is often in the context of the elevation and hard sell of
individual personalities and the boosting and propagation
of their own ministries rather than the genuine serving
and facilitating of ordinary people.

YES!

Miracles and suffering

There was a great earthiness about the miraculous that
you see in the context of the Christian Celtic movement.
There are many examples of the miraculous through
people like Cuthbert. We have come across one example
of when he went to a woman who had lost one child with
the plague and who had another dying. He kissed the
child and then prophesied a healing which the child duly

received. In this kind of story there is a tremendous sense of God's intervention and his meeting people supernaturally at the point of their greatest need. The following two accounts of the miraculous in the life of Columba further amplify this point.

At another time also, when the saint was travelling across the Spine of Britain, one of his companions, a young man named Finten, was afflicted with a sudden sickness and brought to the point of death; and in their grief his fellow soldiers begged the saint to pray for him. In compassion for them he at once held out his holy hands towards heaven in earnest prayer, blessed the sick man, and said, 'This youth for whom you plead will live a long life, and will survive after the death of all of us who are here present, to die in a good old age.'

This prophecy of the blessed man was completely fulfilled in every particular. For the same young man, who afterwards was the founder of the monastery called Cailli aufinde, ended this present life in a good old age.[5]

At the time when Saint Columba was staying for some days in the province of the Picts, a certain layman with his whole household heard the word of life through an interpreter as the saint preached, and believed; and believing, he was baptised, the husband with his wife, children and servants. And after the interval of but a few days, one of the sons of the father of the house was seized by a severe sickness and brought to the very boundary that separates death from life. When the druids saw him dying, they began to mock the parents with loud reproaches, and to exalt their own gods as the more powerful, while disparaging the God of the Christians as the weaker.

When the blessed man was told of all this, roused with zeal for God he went with his companions to the house of his layman friend, where the parents were carrying out the sad

---

[5] Marsden, *The Illustrated Life of Columba*, p. 157.

obsequies for their child, who had just died. Seeing their great sorrow, the saint spoke words of comfort and encouragement to them, that they might have no doubt of God's omnipotence. And he next questioned them, saying, 'In what resting place is the dead boy's body lying?' The bereaved father then took the saint beneath the sad roof, and he entered the place of mourning alone, leaving the attendant throng outside. At once he knelt, and with tears streaming down his face prayed to Christ the Lord; and then rising from his knees he turned his eyes to the one that was dead, saying, 'In the name of the Lord Jesus Christ, rise up again, and stand on your feet.' With these noble words of the saint, the soul returned to the body, and he that was dead came back to life and opened his eyes; and the apostolic man held out his hand and lifted him up, and holding him steady on his feet led him out of the house, and returned him alive again to his parents. Then a shout rose up from the people, lamentation was turned into joy, and the God of the Christians was glorified.

In this miracle of the raising of the dead, let our Columba be accredited with the same power as the prophets Elijah and Elisha, and have a like share of honour with the apostles Peter, Paul and John and among them both, the companies of the prophets and of the apostles, may this prophetic and apostolic man receive a place of honour for all eternity in the land of heaven, with Christ who reigns with the Father in the unity of the Holy Spirit for ever and ever.[6]

This is not to say the Celtic approach lacked realism. While they prayed for God's supernatural involvement they also recognised medicine as a gift from God and embraced it in their lifestyle and practice. Furthermore, this breaking in of the healing power of God was within a broader culture of tremendous suffering and hardship. There are examples of whole groups of monks being

---

[6] Marsden, *The Illustrated Life of Columba*, pp. 157–158.

wiped out through the plague and killed by marauding raiders, as well as many other pains and pitfalls.

As such their experience of the supernatural and God's breaking in does not carry a sense of empty triumphalism. Anybody who lives in the real world will soon have any naive triumphalism dealt with. Faith has many contradictions. Some people get healed and others do not. Some prayers are answered, while others appear not to be. We can theologise, triumphalise and positively confess all we like. The fact remains that people have many deep questions. If our spirituality prevents people from asking these deep-seated questions and expressing their doubts in an environment of faith and openness, we will find that, rather than preparing the church as a bride for union with the living Christ, we are actually preparing our people for disillusionment, a nervous breakdown and burn-out!

Within this there is a lesson for humanity relating to the lordship of Christ. Even in the so-called developed world we cannot deny our human frailty and fallenness. Scientific developments, genetic discoveries and economic pension plans cannot safeguard us. As we discover vaccinations and cures for one set of diseases, other more virulent and mysterious afflictions emerge, often linked to humanity's abuse of our environment and each other. These include the much publicised CJD, AIDS, MS and flesh-rotting viruses, not to mention the more common but just as devastating cancer and heart disease. As Christians, short of an early second coming of the Lord Jesus, we will all inevitably die! This is what the gospel is all about. Resurrection, eternity and death losing its sting.

We have the promise of God's blessing in the land of the living and the expectation of his healing and protection. Yet this is not the whole picture. Neither prophets nor kings, nor anyone else is immune from either

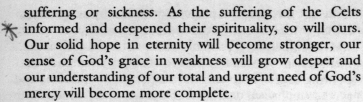

suffering or sickness. As the suffering of the Celts informed and deepened their spirituality, so will ours. Our solid hope in eternity will become stronger, our sense of God's grace in weakness will grow deeper and our understanding of our total and urgent need of God's mercy will become more complete.

Relevant spirituality will need to express a down-to-earth and living experience of God's power breaking out in lifestyle, while recognising that Jesus modelled not just spiritual power, but also in a real sense a living experience of disillusionment, pain and suffering. God is not disengaged from our pain and he identifies with us in our suffering. Thus, in the experience of suffering, there is the opportunity to learn and embrace more of the living God – his very nature – and also to identify more with those around in a truly human way. In this the theology of hope for eternity is every bit as important as faith for the Lord to deliver in the present.

Prophecy

Within the church today there has been much controversy relating to prophecy and the prophetic. We need good teaching on the nature of prophecy and how it can be interpreted, weighed and honoured in the context of the Christian community.

We get the feeling that some people in the church would rather that prophecy just disappeared. It doesn't fit into their inherited theological grid. By contrast, the changes in our culture mean that increasing numbers of people outside the church are far less sceptical, more interested and open to the prophetic. We were amazed to see that a recent edition of the news and current affairs programme *Newsnight* had a long report relating to the

'Sowing the Seeds of Revival' meetings in Marsham Street, Westminster. In the programme they covered the well-documented prophecy from a respected church member in Sheffield which foretold the national out-pouring of grief following the death of Princess Diana and predicted a move of God in the heart of the nation. The report was well balanced and certainly not overtly nega-tive. The fact that a prophecy is now news shows that times are changing. Wake up, church!

Fortunately, the New Testament doesn't enable us to dismiss prophecy and in the Celtic Christians we encounter a movement that had a living and ongoing experience of it.

While praying in the woods Patrick heard the voice of the Irish coming from the air, 'Holy boy, we are asking you to come and work among us again.' He also had a dream of a great rock falling on him, pushing him to the ground and he saw this as a sign of demonic resistance which needed breaking.

Columba, often lauded as a great penitent and a king-maker, is also to be seen as a remarkable prophet. John Marsden's book, *The Illustrated Life of Columba* (a trans-lation of Adamnan's *Vita Columbae*), records numerous examples of Columba's experience of the supernatural and also recalls large numbers of his prophecies, many of which had direct fulfilment. Columba's prophecy relating to the sons of King Aidan is one example of this:

> At another time before the above-mentioned battle the saint asked King Aidan about the succession to the throne. When he replied that he did not know which of his three sons Artuir, Echoid Find, or Domingart, would be king, the saint then spoke as follows: 'None of these three will be king, for they will fall in battle, slain by their enemies. But now, if you have others who are younger, let them come to me, and the

one whom the Lord has chosen from them to be king will at
once rush upon my lap.' When they were called Echoid
Buide, in accordance with the saint's word, came and rested
on his lap. At once the saint blessed and kissed him; and he
said to his father, 'This is the one who will survive and reign
as king after you, and his sons will reign after him.' All these
things came to pass afterwards in their own time, in complete
fulfilment of his words. For Artuir and Echoid Find not long
after were slain in the battle of the Miathi. Domingart was
routed in battle and killed in the land of the Saxons. And
Echoid Buide succeeded to the throne after his father.[7]

There are records of waking visions. These reflect the fact
that there was a very thin veil, in their thinking, separating
the spiritual realm from the earthly realm. Another
example from Columba's life portrays the point effectively:

At another time, while the blessed man was living on the
island of Iou, one day his holy face suddenly lit up with a
wonderfully cheerful and joyous expression; and he raised his
eyes to heaven, overjoyed and filled with gladness beyond
compare. Then, after a brief moment's pause, that sweet and
delightful feeling of joy changed to sadness and sorrow. Two
men, who were standing at that time at the door of his hut,
which was built on higher ground, shared his great sadness
themselves, and asked him the reason for his sudden joyful-
ness and the ensuing sorrow. One of them was Lugne mocu-
Blai, and the other was called Pilu the Saxon. The saint spoke
to them as follows: 'Go in peace, and do not ask that the
reason for that joy, or that sadness either, be revealed by me
now.'

They wept at this, and kneeling down, with their faces
bowed to the ground, they humbly begged him to allow
them some knowledge of what had been revealed to the saint

_____
[7] pp. 81, 84.

in that hour. Seeing their great sadness, he said, 'Because I love you, I would not make you sad. You must first promise me not to betray to any man during my life the secret of which you ask.' They at once promised readily according to his command; and after this promise the venerable man addressed them as follows: 'This present day marks the completion of thirty years of my pilgrimage in Britain. Meanwhile, for many days past I have devoutly begged my Lord to release me from my sojourn here at the end of this present thirtieth year, and summon me at once to the country of heaven. And this was the reason for my joy, about which you question me in your sorrow. For I saw holy angels, sent from the throne on high, coming to meet me to conduct my soul from the flesh. But see now, they are suddenly held back and stay behind our island's Sound on a rock, wishing to come near to summon me from the body, but forbidden to approach closer; and soon they will return to highest heaven. For what the Lord granted to me when I asked with all my strength, that today I might pass from the world to Him, He has altered more swiftly than words, preferring rather to answer the prayers of many churches on my behalf. And to the prayers of those churches it has been granted by the Lord, though against my wish, that I should live on in the flesh for four further years from this day. This delay, so sorrowful for me, was the good reason for my sadness today. When these four remaining years in this life have ended, by God's favour I shall depart happy to the Lord; and I shall depart suddenly, after no bodily affliction, with the holy angels who will come to meet me at that time.' In accordance with these words, which we are told he spoke with deep groans of sorrow and streams of tears, the venerable man lived on in the flesh for four years afterwards.[8]

In our culture we find it much easier to engage with the material, and more difficult to imagine and believe that

---

[8] pp. 208–209.

the invisible realm can dynamically and naturally interact with us in a tangible way. However, within the Celtic culture this was no problem. This provides us with a significant challenge today. We believe God is restoring to the church people who are increasingly more comfortable with the reality of seeing God moving very tangibly and supernaturally. Many people we know are having regular dreams, visions and also angelic visitations which at times are opening up the opportunity for God's kingdom to progress very significantly.

Recently we encountered a situation where a mature Christian woman had been experiencing a great deal of depression and difficulty over a protracted period of time. This had been addressed through prayer, counselling and medication, but it seemed nothing could help. She went to see a well-known Christian leader who then had a waking vision of this woman as a child sitting in the home of a woman who was massaging the child's feet and speaking over her. Immediately the woman recounted that she had spent much of her childhood in Africa and that her mother, on more than one occasion, had taken her into the presence of African 'healers' to be 'blessed'. Clearly a curse had been spoken over her. Once this problem had been identified the person concerned was prayed for and a remarkable healing and deliverance took place.

We could recount numerous other stories of direct visions and prophetic words relating to individuals and churches which have proved to be both accurate and significant in the opening up of these situations to the life and love of Jesus and the gospel. An encounter with the supernatural working of God changes our perspectives.

The Celts had a great love of Scripture and a real desire for it. They loved every aspect of its teachings, but it would be fair to say that they appear to have had a particular empathy and love for the Book of John. They loved his spiritual insight and called him 'the eagle'. As they prayed, they longed to soar like eagles into the heavenly realms, where spiritual insight and discernment could be attained. They felt that as they moved to this height in God's Spirit they, like the eagle, would have an overview of the land below and would be able to see the enemy as potential prey. In this respect the Celts often talked about the 'eagle eye' in prayer – the ability to see through what is going on in the natural realm to the supernatural and to perceive what is happening 'behind the scenes' in order that they could respond accordingly. Much of the apocalyptic literature in Scripture has this type of feel to it, particularly the Book of Revelation written by John himself.

A passion for Scripture and experience

The Celtic Christians had a richly holistic spirituality which challenges the dualism and one-dimensional spirituality of our age. There was a balanced concern for scholarship, the Bible and spirituality. It was led by a strong Trinitarian theology and a wonderfully holistic approach to worship and art. Their worship included many different facets and was rich in symbolism. We highlight these aspects not to endorse superstition, but to exhort us towards greater depths in our walk with God. We are saddened that in our incredibly noisy and often relentless lifestyle as Christians we are at times afraid to be quiet, to meditate and to experience God's truth as we focus on him.

As Evangelicals and charismatics, often our meetings reflect the frenetic and one-dimensional aspects of society rather than leading people to be fed in an encounter with the living God. We are whole human beings, so in order to perceive God fully it is not a case of us encountering him only with our minds or even just with minds and emotions. There are other senses like smell and taste which can further adorn the body of God's truth. If this were not so, the 'breaking of bread' would not need to be participated in, merely talked about! Furthermore, there is no particular need to retreat into dead expressions of form and tradition that often have plenty of symbolism, but whose symbols have died in the eyes of many.

We believe that in this generation and culture, many churches will have to reassess their attitude towards liturgy and symbolism. In this vein, what we are looking for is not necessarily a regression into past liturgies but an expression of new liturgies and symbols which engage dynamically with contemporary culture while at the same time drawing people to encounter the living and dynamic power of God's Spirit.

As we begin to explore these areas we will open ourselves to both cynicism and misrepresentation. For example, in our own situation a couple of years ago, people began to carry sticks in the context of their worship. For Roger, his own coloured stick of red, white and blue originated from his studies relating to the Celtic Christian movement. He became impressed with the way they used colours symbolically. He encountered the fact that often red, for them, was the colour of blood martyrdom – the laying down of one's very life and life-blood to follow Jesus. Following on, the colour white symbolised the denial of one's own agenda and lifestyle in order to be fully taken up with following Jesus. The colour blue for them symbolised the crucifying of the sinful nature and 'dying to self'.

This symbolism seemed especially poignant to Roger,

so he made a stick of the three colours which he carried around in the context of worship. As he prayed, observing and touching the various colours, he could be engaging and focusing on the cross of Jesus, his shed blood and other aspects of the symbolism. For a period the carrying of the stick symbolised some key things that God was impressing upon Roger's heart and life.

At times we have overheard a measure of cynicism relating to 'sticks', and criticism at the assumed shallowness of such symbols. Our view is that a symbol is merely a symbol. There are perhaps as many sticks in Scripture as there are candles! A stick has the potential to be both profound and vacuous, as can a candle or any other form of symbolism. In fact sticks aren't the issue. We were stunned to find various people across the body of Christ having theological discussions over sticks and their nature. The fact is that months afterwards people were still talking about sticks when in actual fact by that time you would be hard pushed to find so much as a twig in any of our meetings! Sticks were not the issue. It was the beginning for us of finding new and often transitory symbols (more in keeping with the post-modern mindset) to help us as churches and individuals to engage more deeply with God. As the prophetic times and seasons of the church ebb and flow alongside the changes in our communities, so our symbols need to be remixed, changed and often reinterpreted.

Therefore in our everyday lives we need to be looking at fashion, clothing and other areas of symbolism to help people reflect on God's truth on an ongoing basis. Rather than wearing sackcloth and ashes, perhaps contemporary clothing and jewellery could be designed which symbolises devotion to God. Then when, for example, our people go out into clubland they will carry some symbols which not only provide them with a reminder of God's hand upon their lives, but also with some potential conversation starters.

Worship and prayer

Celtic Christians appear to have had a rich appreciation of culture and art. To them work was sacred. As they walked they prayed. They crossed themselves, they symbolically drew circles around as they prayed for protection. Their prayers encompassed the rhythm of life and were very earthy. They had prayers for getting up, dressing, working, resting, meeting friends, cooking, tidying the house, undressing and going to bed. They were deeply influenced by Scripture, as well as being Christ-centred, but symbolism was part of their lives.

We find this profoundly challenging. Every aspect of life, every day, filled with a sense of spiritual significance and also lived in a way that is conscious of God's love and provision. More liturgical expressions of Christianity try to incorporate this by having various offices and services throughout the day. It would be fair to say that while we appreciate the heart behind this approach, this is alien to our culture and ecclesiology. Furthermore, the last thing we would want to end up with is a kind of ritual-bound religiosity. For example, there is something strange about saying prayers of grace before meals after we have been praying for two hours together, and are actually in an environment of thankfulness! Or, indeed, prayers of thanksgiving before meals when actually people are completely traumatised because the food they are about to eat looks more like a cremated ferret than something which inspires praise to the living God! In fact a prayer for mercy rather than thanksgiving may be more appropriate! We are greatly attracted to the table grace that is traditionally associated with Brigid and her community which was famous for its hospitality:

> I should like a great lake of finest ale
> For the King of kings.
> I should like a table of the choicest food
> For the family of heaven.
> Let the ale be made from the fruits of faith,
> And the food be forgiving love.
>
> I should welcome the poor to my feast,
> For they are God's children.
> I should welcome the sick to my feast,
> For they are God's joy.
> Let the poor sit with Jesus at the highest place,
> And the sick dance with the angels.
>
> God bless the poor,
> God bless the sick,
> And bless our human race.
> God bless our food,
> God bless our drink,
> All homes, O God, embrace.[9]

How do we bring a sense of thanksgiving and wholeness into our lifestyle? How do we bring a sense of thanksgiving and prayer into the everyday and mundane areas of life? How do we help people encounter the living presence of God in an ongoing way? How do we help people express a Jesus-centred and scripturally orientated sense of lifestyle in all they are doing? These are questions that we need to be asking at this moment in time if we are really going to help our people towards an experience of the living God in everyday life.

The Celtic Christians' prayer life shows a balance

---

[9] Cahill, *How the Irish Saved Civilisation*, pp. 174–175.

through many different approaches. It would appear that charismatic, ecstatic and aggressive noisy battle prayers were usual. There was also a clear emphasis on silence and stillness. At times their lives were very austere with fasting and prayer. The Celts went to remote places for spiritual retreat, sometimes for short periods, sometimes for years.

We believe that there is much we can learn from this. In one sense a book could be written about every one of these observations. However, if we can encourage a healthy rhythm of aggression and activity contrasted with silence and stillness; of fasting contrasted with feasting; and spiritual service and exertion contrasted with retreat and soaking in God's presence, then we believe that we would be far more whole and less impoverished in our spirituality.

There are many accounts of some interesting disciplines to aid prayer. Patrick prayed in the frost and cold to keep him awake. Cuthbert and Melrose went up to their armpits in freezing cold sea so that they could pray through the night and stay awake. While we are not necessarily advocating walking into the North Sea (the summer is bad enough, let alone in winter!), encounters with the wild beauty of God's natural creation can inspire us in our prayer and devotion.

Some of Roger's greatest encounters with the love of Jesus have been while fishing. He remembers one particular occasion fishing on an island in the middle of a four-mile-long lake in Holland in the midst of a storm. It had rained for three days and nights and was extremely muddy. He had been alone for long periods and it was about 11 o'clock in the evening when for the first time the sky had partially cleared. Sitting outside drinking a cup of tea, he could see a mixture of the stars, the moon and angry, billowing clouds. The noise of the wind through the trees was deafening. He stood up and leaned into the wind and continued praying and thanking God for his wild power and dynamic nature. At that moment the sense of God's peace, the infilling of the Holy Spirit and his joy, was so strong and powerful that Roger could scarcely stand up. Tears poured down his cheeks and he had to sit down and try to compose himself when one of his Dutch non-Christian friends from the other side of the island came to visit. Roger had not been smoking marijuana like they had, but it would be fair to say that he had been having a lot more fun!

The hermit instinct

Within the Celtic tradition hermits lived out a full life which most Christians couldn't. As they lived in isolation and often incredible poverty, they became a prophetic focus. Carrying out continuing prayer and intercession, they became an anchor to the communities. They protected very busy monasteries from losing the emphasis on spirituality. We are not sure how we incorporate this dynamic today, but we are sure that we need it!

We are aware of people within our own church community who display elements of the hermit instinct. These are people who are giving their lives over to prayer, intercession and encountering God. Some people are more at home in these areas. They are made for retreat and God's presence. Their input to the community and to individuals has been significant and their urge to retreat and to be with God has been an exhortation and encouragement to the heart of our church. We believe most traditions have such people – people who are either more advanced in years, or people who have a measure of maturity and gifting in God which means that other individuals of all ages will go to see them, be with them and receive their prayer and often prophetic wisdom. We know of such individuals within evangelicalism who would probably not see themselves as flowing out of the hermit tradition!

Symbolism and imagination

Rather like the post-modern age the Celtic church had many symbols. It had a way of converting or reinterpreting pagan symbols. For example, the knot which was the pagan symbol for the endless cycle of existence became the symbol for eternity. Within this symbolism was a great deal of scholarly and biblical research. The Celts had many great Old and New Testament biblical scholars and some notable theologians. This symbolism gave a rich dynamic to their spirituality and, as we have already observed, it gave them many vehicles through which to engage the broader culture around them.

Within this symbolism there was a tremendous sense of imagination. They perceived God with all of their senses and appeared not to degrade either the intellect or the emotions. Much of their communication came through symbols. Many of their statements of faith were expressed in carvings as well as within written manuscripts. Drawings and symbols were used rather than concepts. The Trinity has often been described as like ice, steam and water. Patrick's famous illustration was to explain the Trinity by using the shamrock. They planted crosses all over the place, situating them on pagan sites to describe symbolically the power of the gospel.

Mystery

We would strongly emphasise that Christianity is not a 'mystery religion'. The Book of Colossians reveals that

Christ is in fact the 'mystery' and we, through salvation, are in on the secrets. However, God's ways are higher than our ways and his thoughts are higher than our thoughts (Is 55:9). As finite human beings it is impossible for us fully to understand and perceive everything about God with our rational minds. We must continue rationally to formulate, teach and emphasise the importance of engaging the brain to grasp God's objective truth. However, if our spirituality is restricted to an intellectual exercise and the living Lord is boxed into our particular systematic theology, then we cease to do him justice.

The love, grace and authority of the living God are at the same time understandable and also beautiful mysteries which can be further encountered through the creative, the symbolic and through our senses. Often as Evangelicals we 'kill off' worship by ensuring that everything is defined, controlled, scripted and boxed in. We seem afraid to express that we neither know everything nor understand everything. Confessing and celebrating this fact doesn't make the living God any less real. In fact it comes as a relief to many believers who, while they have an intimate relationship with the Lord on one hand, find many aspects of his glory hard to perceive and contain. And quite rightly so, for they are only human!

In this culture we believe we will again need to use the poetic and the visual. We are encouraging many people to begin to explore and demonstrate their spirituality through the use of the creative arts. As we have done this in the context of the church we have been aware of different people involved in sculpture, pottery, various forms of artwork, fashion and other areas of creativity. We have encouraged them to use these idioms to portray their faith and to stimulate a questioning hunger. In these areas the last things we are looking for are pictures of doves flying all over the place and dramas where people get saved at the end! We are looking to stimulate a more challenging and indigenous grass-roots expression of our hunger for God portraying different aspects of his glory.

Also, at times, within the context of our worship meetings, we have encouraged artists to come and draw what they feel is happening as the church worships together. We have also had sculptors and even potters working to one side of the meeting. Sometimes, in the process of the worship the artists are encouraged to interpret what it is they are portraying. At other times the work is left to stand in its own right and people are invited to go and view it at the end and ask the Holy Spirit to speak to them.

These experiments have been well received by visitors, who have been stimulated and challenged as well as surprised by the creativity. Furthermore, some of our church members who are not particularly turned on by singing or engaged by some of the more monochrome expressions of worship have found a fresh stimulation and outlet for their Jesus-inspired creativity.

There has been fresh vision and edge among the creative and more prophetic people in the church community who have now been allowed to come to the forefront. As a result, on a good day, our corporate worship expression as a church reflects the heart and gifts of people right across the community and also has a greater level of creativity and depth about it.

7

Spirituality 2 – A New Rhythm in Lifestyle

The Celtic Christians were aware of rhythm. Rhythm in nature; rhythm in the body. The body ages and changes. Their culture would have been far more at ease with this process than ours. Age and maturity were to be respected and honoured. In our society we seem to be trying to deny this process. There is often an alienation between young and old, and our culture encourages an 'ostrich' approach towards aging. The whole cosmetic industry, with its operations, creams and other profit-making scams, is built around the myth of 'eternal youth' and it preys on the fear of aging. As we get older we should look forward to enjoying the benefits of experience. There should be honour in aging and a sense of growing closer to the glory of eternity and heaven.

Their sense of rhythm meant the Celts saw the seasons and work such as weaving, reaping, men rowing together and women walking together as opportunities for worship and prayer. They sang songs of worship to God along with the rhythm of the waves. Today, we have lost the sense of rhythms in our fractured society which has been depersonalised by technology. Western rationalism has cut us off from our spiritual roots. However, there is a new rhythm. It is the old rhythm recycled. It is the rhythm of Jesus – Redeemer and Creator.

The new rhythm

God wants to refresh our spirituality so that it consists of more than just a few power encounters with the Holy Spirit and regular meetings, but involves the bringing of his heart, life and word into the depths of our everyday lives. He is challenging us about the rhythms of our lifestyle, the way we worship him, the way we work, the way we eat, the way we sleep, the pace that we go and the way our lives interlock.

The word 'stress' is often used in our society and this diagnosis is very rarely weighed against a value base. We want to look at 'rhythm' and what it means to have a new rhythm.

Rediscovery

God wants us to rediscover the joy of walking with him and the beauty of what it means to be a follower of Christ, having his Holy Spirit around us continually. He wants us to rediscover the beauty of what it means to base our lives on God's word and to have our relationships reflect his glory. As we encounter this glory we will be awestruck with who God is, because he is the Creator, the source of all good things. Many of us have been inspired by the Celtic Christian movement because it seemed to bring together a knowledge of Scripture, an experience of Jesus and an encounter with his power. These things interlock in a seamless garment of lifestyle and service to God.

'Rhythm' is just a word, and as such it is nothing to be frightened of. We often use the word 'radical' to describe

Christianity. That word is not part of the Bible's regular language, but most of us would say that Jesus' teaching takes us back to the root of our lives and identity – that is all that 'radical' means. 'Rhythm' is another word just like 'radical'. 'Radical' describes the kingdom of God and 'rhythm' describes the nature of God – what it means to move with him and flow with his purposes. It describes a biblical spirituality of prayer and giving.

Dictionaries reveal that rhythm expresses itself in word, music, arts, painting, sculpture and lifestyle. The meaning encompasses the movement of words and phrases in prose and verse. It encompasses the rhythm of music, beats, verses and stanzas. Within the arts and sculpture it encompasses the contrast between shapes, colours, light and dark. It also applies to life – getting up, walking, moving, the way our bodies operate. It is a physiological word and it is used in physics and science to analyse what is going on in the created realm.

The God of rhythm

As you look at creation you see that God is a God of rhythm. Right at the beginning, in Genesis 1:14, God says, 'Let there be lights in the expanse of the sky to separate the day from the night, and let them serve as signs to mark seasons and days and years, and let them be lights in the expanse of the sky to give light on the earth.' And it was so.

God made the earth and everything in it. He is the God of creation, colour, light and beauty. As he looks at humanity, he loves us because to him we are the pinnacle of his creation. To him we are far more beautiful than anything else he has made. He wants us to live in harmony with him, to know him.

God has given us time and he wants to flow alongside us in our lives. He is not sitting in heaven disconnected, disengaged and detached from us like a cosmic dictator or an absentee landlord. God is with us, he relates to us, he is alongside us as our lives in this world go through summer, autumn, winter and spring. The seasons express something of the spirituality that God wants us to live in: 'To everything there is a season, a time for every purpose under heaven' (Ecc 3:1, New King James Version).

In the eighteenth century – the age of reason – theologians struggled to grasp how God relates to his world. Is he 'out there' or is he 'down here' among us? They concluded that God is both *transcendent* (separate and far above) and also *immanent* (very much present in his creation). Dead religion and rationalism always over-emphasise the transcendent distance of God from us, whereas the more dynamic and holistic expressions of Christianity also major on Christ's immanence. God is in the seasons. He is the hand within the glove of creation for 'in him all things hold together' (Col 1:17).

The Jews well understood this balance and their community life had its various seasons. There was circumcision at birth and bar mitzvah at coming of age, as a benchmark of entry into the community as each person grew from childhood into adulthood. As they grew and matured so their experience of the seasons and other areas of their growth were marked by the festivals and acts of worship which were an integral part of the Old Covenant.

We are also created as human beings to worship and to express this worship in lifestyle. As we look at Scripture we realise it is full of worship. Worship is not something we do on Sunday or merely a song that we sing. The reason why the Christian lifestyle was so attractive to the pagan Celts was because they saw that it fulfilled all of their aspirations to be whole people. As they looked at the Christian Celts they saw a powerful and real expression of the living God. When Paul went into the Areopagus in Acts 17, the gospel impressed some of those present because the people who were spiritually seeking could see that the truth of Jesus made everything fit together.

Biblical rhythms

We see that there are many rhythms in Scripture. The Jews had a Sabbath day, a day that is one in seven. Leviticus provides for a Sabbath year, a year in seven. After seven Sabbath years there was to be a Jubilee year, which is one in fifty. For fifty years people made money, bought land and accumulated wealth, and at the end of fifty years they gave everything back to the original owners to prevent an unjust gap between the rich and poor. So there was a rhythm that was one in seven and a rhythm that was one in fifty.

In the New Testament we see that Christ is our Sabbath (Heb 4). We don't live under the laws of the Old Testament rhythms, but Christ is our Sabbath and it is in him that we live and move and have our being. In Christ everything holds together: all of the cosmic realm, all of creation, every human being. If we want to hold together it is in Christ that we will endure. It is through his death and resurrection, through the ongoing flow of his rhythm, and the filling of his Spirit that we will hold together and will learn to live as God intends.

In Scripture, lifestyle is full of meaning and of walking with God. Work, despite the curse of the Fall, was a blessing. Genesis records God giving us work as a blessing because we need to create, to be active and to be fulfilled. We are created to express our emotions and creativity, to exercise and exhaust our minds, bodies and artistic inclinations; to have fun. In Scripture there are many ways that God's people did this through their offerings and worship. They gave their 'first-fruits'. When the seasons came and the crops matured, the first and best crops were always given to God. In our lifestyles part of our rhythm should be the giving of first-fruits. The best wine, the first-fruits of our finances, the best of our lives, the best of our hearts, goes to God.

The Book of Lamentations is a very sad book which weeps from beginning to end, but right in the middle of the sadness and mourning is God's rhythm, where the writer says that the mercies of God are new every morning (Lam 3:22–24). No matter how bad or painful things are, no matter how much in exile we feel, the rhythm of God is fresh and new every morning. Every morning God's forgiveness and life and Spirit come to us and wash us afresh, so there are daily rhythms.

There is something so profound in Solomon's famous passage in Ecclesiastes 3 about the seasons of life: 'A time to weep and a time to laugh, a time to mourn and a time to dance, a time to scatter stones and a time to gather them . . . a time to keep and a time to throw away . . . a time to be silent and a time to speak' (vv. 4–5a, 6b, 7b). For Chris, much of 1996 was a time of weeping, mourning and silence. After ten hectic and happy years in leadership he hit burn-out, described medically as 'exhaustion'. At this time he did not preach for months. He asked many questions about his calling, his place and the fruitfulness of his labours. The burn-out was about more than overwork. Rather God created a season to help Chris to understand what was to be scattered and thrown away, and what was to be kept and gathered. During a long period of rest, recovery and gradual restoration,

Chris has learned much about himself, and the season of laughter and dancing is returning.

As Evangelicals we perhaps give rather too much credit to the devil for suffering. Winter is not from the devil. The seasons are part of God's good creation and so are the seasons in our lives.

As you look at the Bible you see that lifestyle is impregnated with worship, family, relationships, morality and ethics. God's order is there. There is an old hymn which comes from Psalm 29:2 – 'Worship the Lord in the splendour of his holiness.' This splendour of holiness carries the sense of an environment which has an order about it. When God's rhythm comes into our lives it brings an order of truth, morality, integrity and creativity. An order which puts us in contact with who we are.

However, this is not a controlling, institutional, oppressive or repressive order, but one that releases and frees us to become love slaves of Jesus.

A rhythm of freedom

At the end of the film *Braveheart*, when William Wallace is dying, he is offered drugs to alleviate his pain, but he refuses them because he wants to hold on to his mind. He says, 'Everybody has to die, but not many people actually live.' At the moment of his death, he cries out, '*Freedom*!' We believe this communicates something of the heart of God, because the rhythm of God is freedom. The rhythm of God frees us to live so that we can walk through our lives with Jesus, knowing his word, crying 'freedom' as we go through. God is a God of rhythms and we believe he wants our lives to be centred around Jesus. This sense of the Lord being present through all the rhythms of life permeated the

worship of the Christian Celts, as these words from the
Carmina Gadelica reveal.

> The eye of the great God,
> The eye of the God of glory,
> The eye of the King of hosts,
> The eye of the King of the living,
> Pouring upon us
> At each time and season,
> Pouring upon us
> Gently and generously.
> Glory to thee,
> Thou glorious sun.
>
> Glory to thee, the sun,
> Face of the God of life.
>
> *Carmina Gadelica*[1]

A Jesus-centred rhythm

Romans 12:1–2 exhorts us not to allow ourselves to be
squeezed into the pattern or rhythm of the world, but to
be transformed by the renewing of our minds. Let us
allow the whole of our lives to become worship. As we do
this we will know God's will because we are no longer
flowing with the rhythm of the world but with the rhythm
of God, his Holy Spirit and the rhythm of Scripture.

   In Matthew 6:5–15 the prayer Jesus gives reveals a
rhythm of life, a rhythm of loving God and seeking first
God's kingdom, of giving generously to others and forgiving others, because if we don't the channel of God's
forgiveness to us is blocked. This prayer reveals the heart
of a rhythm of walking with God. If we want to find
freedom in the context of our society we need to allow

---

[1] Anthony Duncan, *Celtic Christianity* (Element Books, 1992).

the rhythm of this prayer to influence us. Loving, seeking, giving and forgiving will be the keys which characterise us and should encapsulate our lifestyle.

For many of us our lives are characterised by tension, unforgiveness, bitterness and unresolved relationship problems which reflect a broken, destructive rhythm. God wants to bring us to his word and put something right at the very depths of our lives which will transform us. The rhythm of Jesus is the rhythm of the kingdom of God. In Matthew 5–7 we see different aspects that are key if we want to be attractive as a believing community to those who are seeking to know God and find heaven and eternal life. Our attractiveness will revolve around us having the kingdom of God right at the heart of both our community and personal value systems.

The thrust of Jesus' teaching says that if you want to be stress-free then love your neighbour as you love yourself. Lay down your life for others. If someone asks you to carry one thing, carry two. If someone wants you to go half a mile, go a mile with them. Be a servant, deny yourself. Right at the heart of the kingdom is a relational rhythm which has a core of friendship and relationship. All relationships rely on the Holy Spirit and his flow to keep us one and in unity and identity together, while loving our neighbours.

A fear-free rhythm

The rhythm of the kingdom is also a fear-free rhythm. Society is full of fears. People are desperately running after money, treasures, success and significance through what they own, the car they drive, whether or not they have promotion, how good they are, what others think of them. These are the tensions they live under; the desire to acquire more and more stuff. As someone said, 'I've been freed from stuff because I haven't got anything except for two bin liners that are in America, and I'm here!'

God wants us to have a fear-free rhythm and to live now in the light of eternity. Jesus said that our treasures should be in heaven (Mt 6:19–21). If you focus on God and seek first his kingdom, then you become like the birds, which just get on with their lives free from fear and worry. In Matthew 6:25–26 Jesus tells us to be like the birds. Rather than worrying about what we are going to eat, we should instead have our priority focused in other areas.

Perhaps Jesus pointed to birds because they are so diverse and yet so sensitive, through their instinctive drives, to the rhythms and seasons of creation. For example, some families of birds like the starlings or the sparrows are resident in the same place throughout the year. Others, like the swallows and the terns, migrate thousands of miles across oceans and continents twice a year. The Celts saw the connection, using the migrating Barnacle Goose as their symbol for the Holy Spirit. With birds there is a time for courtship, a time for nest-building, a time for feeding and a time for singing. They do this without fear or effort and seemingly at times with an unrestrained joy. Think about this when you next get woken up by a blackbird singing its praises to God!

God wants to break us out of the fear mentality in our society into a fear-free rhythm where we are not driven by greed or by other negative emotions but we are led by the Holy Spirit into the peace of God and an experience of his wholeness.

Rhythm of community

The Jesus rhythm is a community rhythm. The New Testament exhorts us not to give up the habit of meeting

together (Heb 10:25). Jesus gathered his disciples together in twos and threes and when they broke bread they
weren't in a formal meeting kneeling at an altar. They
would have been reclining, laying down at the table,
drinking, in relationship.

The rhythm of Jesus is not a lonely rhythm but one that
recognises that human beings are created for relationships and friendships. God is Father, Son and Holy Spirit
– one yet three. He is a relational God. God has created
us for relationship with him and one another. As a church
we want to find the love and community and oneness of
God. We are a community of faith. We are followers of
Jesus responding to the rhythm of Jesus and the flow of
the Holy Spirit.

There is so much for us to explore and experiment with
in these areas. What does it mean to live in community in
this culture? In what way can the Celtic monastic models
influence our churches today? How can we model the
sharing of lives, resources and family together in an
increasingly fragmented society? How can we be a radical
community living for justice and rights in our age? We
have few answers, only experiments, and there are probably many diverse ways of addressing these issues.
However, in Appendix 2 we document a little of our own
journey as a church.

Broken rhythms

All of us live under broken rhythms. Our lifestyle
becomes fractured and stressed for both good and bad
reasons. We live in a world where there is sin, tension and
pain. The foot of the cross comes into that tension and
pressure, and brings the cleansing blood of Jesus to
us. We may feel broken and out of sorts in different areas

Worship

of our lives, but God's word, in the words of the psalmist, is light to our eyes and honey to our lips. We may feel that our taste has gone, life has lost its flavour and our eyes have become darkened. Material things no longer satisfy us. However, when the word of God comes it brings light to our eyes and a beautiful taste to our lips, setting us on fire again.

We live in a society where people's eyes no longer sparkle and whose taste has been destroyed by misuse and abuse. We have been assaulted by materialism, the breakdown of community, family and identity.

There are many reasons why rhythms break down. For instance, there is sin. Sin, both corporately and individually, brings brokenness in relationships and separates people from God. There is a cry from people who are living in sin – a cry right from their depths to be saved, set free, to know what it is to be loved and have an answer to their brokenness and fractured relationships. The cross goes to the depths of these issues. If we are in sin we will be stressed. Let's not call sin stress; let's call it sin. The way out is by repentance, not therapy. We must encourage people to turn to God and turn away from sin, entering a partnership together with the Lord Jesus Christ which will enable them gradually to reconstruct their lives.

The world system breaks our rhythms. Greed; the God of success; companies that own people. They want to be the priority over family life, relationships and spirituality. The gods of this world put pressure on people to break them away from God. We are in a world system, attempting to live in the world but not of it, and that is the tension. Many of us are living this way, day in day out, at work. The rhythm of God is not to back off and lock ourselves away. It leads us to be in this world while challenging us to allow the Holy Spirit to pour out and break in, keeping us safe from pollution and compromise in the midst of the corruption around.

Sometimes there are tensions because we are trying to be a Christian in the work place but it's difficult to know how to behave as there seems to be so many 'grey' areas. The process of 'sticking our necks out' and expressing our beliefs and ethics can provoke both opposition and tension. But the words of Jesus encourage us to rejoice when we receive opposition because all the prophets who came before us were treated in the same way (Mt 5:11–12). Don't back off, because that will bring stress of a different type. Go for it and receive the grace, mercy and promises of God as you go.

Spiritual conflicts

Spiritual conflicts at times interrupt our walk with God. Jesus didn't come to bring peace but to bring a sword. When the gospel comes it will often bring polarisation between light and dark. That is why Jesus had to be crucified. Religion and the rulers couldn't handle him because he was so full of light and they were living in darkness. Spiritual warfare is often like that. There will be spiritual pressures. We will all be tempted to sin, tempted to be selfish, tempted sexually. God wants to give us the strength to break the power of those things so that we can live in freedom.

We are in a war. The Christian Celts understood this, as we have already said. Iona today is mainly known as a retreat centre, but in those days it was right in the middle of the trading routes between Ireland and Scotland. It was right where the heat was. Kings used to go and enquire, 'Prophet, does the Lord have anything to say to me?' And as we have already observed, one king went to Columba, presenting him with three of his sons, asking, 'Who should we make king?' Being at the centre of activity as we follow Jesus can often bring pressure, responsibilities, tension and challenges.

J. H. Jowett has expressed the cost of all this in one of our favourite pieces of writing:

> The range of our possible sufferings is determined by the largeness and nobility of our aims. It is possible to evade a multitude of sorrows by the cultivation of an insignificant life. Indeed, if it be a man's ambition to avoid the troubles of life the recipe is perfectly simple. Let him shed his ambitions in every direction, let him cut the wings of every soaring purpose, and let him assiduously cultivate a little life, with the fewest correspondences and relations. By this means a whole continent of afflictions will be escaped and will remain unknown.
>
> Cultivate negations and large tracts of the universe will cease to exist. For instance, cultivate deafness and you are saved from the horrors of discords. Cultivate blindness and you are saved from the assault of the ugly. Stupefy a sense and you shut out a world. And therefore it is literally true that if you want to get through the world with the smallest trouble you must reduce yourself to the smallest compass. That is why so many people and even so many professedly Christian people get through life so easily, and with a minimum acquaintance with tribulation. It is because they have reduced their souls to a minimum that their course through the years is not so much the transit of a man as the passage of air amoeba. They have no finely organised nervous system, for they have deadened and arrested the growth of one nerve after another. They have cut the sensitive wires which bind the individual to the race, and they are cosily self-contained and the shuddering sorrow of the world never disturbs their seclusion.[2]

---

[2] J. H. Jowett, *The Price of Enlargement*. The quotation is inspired by 1 Peter 5:10 and Philippians 3:10.

Stress can come because of sacrifice. It has been said that if you don't want to be hurt, never love anybody. But if you choose to love, there is pain. Sometimes things go wrong, people fall away from the Lord, churches fail and disillusionment sets in. However, there is no life without sacrifice. No inspiration and adventure without giving, loving, risk and endurance. Life without these things is really a living death. Without Jesus we are condemned to cynicism, despair, destruction and selfishness while our lives become self-absorbed. But with Jesus we can give ourselves away and learn to live eternal life now as a foretaste of the future.

Restoring rhythms

What does this mean? Who is Lord? Jesus gives us a biblical focus and releases the Holy Spirit as someone who will lead us forward. The Celtic symbol of the wild goose symbolises adventuring with the Holy Spirit. For some of us things are out of control in our lives. We are busy. Our careers represent a tyrannical rule over our lives rather than a vocational journey. Jesus is not Lord, and the 'market forces' dictate. When we go to Jesus there will need to be sacrifice. Sometimes we will need to lay things down in order to find space to go forward.

At other times, our lives will be quite rightly full of the concerns of others, and the demands of our jobs will mean we barely have time to think of ourselves. That is also part of the sacrifice.

However, for some of us things are out of control and God is bringing us into a new rhythm. Churches will need to take this seriously and for many it will involve a complete change in how they operate. We believe God wants to lead us in this as we incarnate our faith in the context of our community. God is leading the church towards new rhythms and approaches.

We believe this is a time for both reflection and change. Some people grasp change as a blessing. That's Holy Spirit, that's biblical, that's Celtic. Others have to be made sick before they will change. It's often like this when people become Christians. Some come to faith easily, but others have to reach rock bottom, where there is no other way and no other door. Malcolm Muggeridge said that if there was another Christ, another faith, another book, another philosophical system, he would have chosen it because he didn't want Christ; he hated Christ and he didn't want to be a Christian. But in the end he had to come to his knees because there is no other book, no other way, no other Christ. There is only Jesus. He couldn't deny it; he had to give his life to God. Sadly, some Christians are a little like that. They need to come completely to the end of themselves before they begin to look humbly for the next step in their journey.

The hunger for a more 'holistic' and fully orbed spirituality more rooted in lifestyle is very deep, both in the church and society at large. Now is the time for us to draw inspiration from the past and 'remix' an orthodox, biblically Christ-centred spirituality which will propel us into the future.

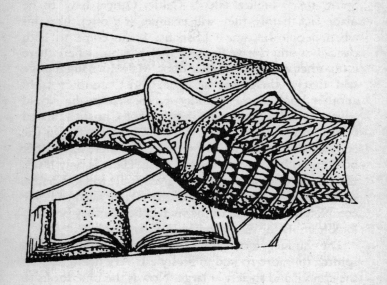

Wild Goose

8

A Sense of Adventure

When we first encountered the Celtic Christian movement one of the things that impacted us with such force was the dynamic sense of adventure that seemed to be at the heart of their spirituality. We were captivated and inspired by the incredible stories of sacrifice and adventure we encountered in the Celtic saints.

Furthermore, there seemed to be a freedom and spontaneity about their service of God which we found profoundly appealing and challenging.

Flowing out of the Celtic communities went the *'peregrinati'* (in our language, the 'wanderers'). Out of a life soaked with prayer these people had an incredible desire to go. It was not unusual that following a time of seeking God's presence they would get into a coracle, cast themselves adrift and see where the waves took them. For them this was a kind of pilgrimage or mission.

One example of this was a group of monks from southern Ireland who got into a coracle with no oars and no proper provisions. They cast themselves adrift and after seven days they arrived in Cornwall and were brought before King Alfred. When asked why they had embarked on this somewhat unusual journey they answered, 'We stole away because we wanted for the love of God to be on pilgrimage and we cared not where.' However, these journeys were not engaged in lightly. They flowed out of a great sense of faith, risk and adventure, as the beautiful prayer of Brendan expresses:

> Shall I abandon, O King of Mysteries, the soft comforts of home? Shall I turn my back on my native land, and my face towards the sea?
>
> Shall I put myself wholly at the mercy of God, without silver, without a horse, without fame and honour? Shall I throw myself wholly on the King of kings, without sword and shield, without food and drink, without a bed to lie on?
>
> Shall I say farewell to my beautiful land, placing myself under Christ's yoke? Shall I pour out my heart to him, confessing my manifold sins and begging forgiveness, tears streaming down my cheeks?
>
> Shall I leave the prints of my knees on the sandy beach, a record of my final prayer in my native land? Shall I then suffer every kind of wound that the sea can inflict?
>
> Shall I take my tiny coracle across the wide, sparkling ocean? O King of the Glorious Heaven, shall I go of my own choice upon the sea?
>
> O Christ, will you help me on the wild waves?[1]

The Celtic instinct was to respond to the dynamic prompting of the Holy Spirit and then to begin adventuring and wandering with Jesus, carrying out evangelism, mission and church-planting as they went. This was pilgrimage to them!

We believe the models offered by these godly men and women can be a great inspiration to us today. Often our churches and our spirituality are governed by an ordered predictability. Any thought of development, change or

---

[1] Mitton, *Restoring the Woven Cord*.

new horizons is responded to with a fear and in-built reserve. Too often our theological thinking has been encapsulated and boxed in by our traditional systems. When what God wants to do becomes too big for our systems we are unable to respond to what he is doing outside of them. We have strait-jacketed ourselves and therefore struggle with anything that doesn't fit within our often restricted mind-set.

Often our prayers become captive to the realm of safety and predictability and lack the passion and desperation which can be fired in our hearts by a sense of adventure and 'going' as we step forward in faith with Jesus. Too often our leadership forums and structures are dominated by strategies, discussions and the attention to mainten-ance. Such things, while often necessary, are not going to fire the church into the future.

The Celtic Christians inspire us into a world of 'God appointments' and chance meetings. The calling of God and the strategic way forward in mission are informed and prompted by visions of God opening and shutting doors supernaturally, rather like we see in the development of the New Testament church (Acts 16:6–10).

The Celts lay down a challenge to us. Are we going to allow the prophetic and inspirational to be right at the heart of our lives? Too often our planning and strategising revolves around the investing of our resources in a 'low interest, safe spiritual bank account' rather than embark-ing on a spiritual bungy-jump into the future, which seems to be more in keeping with the Abrahamic calling of God to go and be used.

As we have already pointed out in previous chapters, the Celtic instinct was not to possess, rule and necessarily settle down, but to move on. Robert Louis Stephenson's phrase, 'Better to travel hopefully than arrive', could in fact be a Celtic motto. Their natural cultural identity often made them fiercely independent and on occasions a little anarchic. This wild determination to go for God offered a considerable provocation and challenge to the church as it already existed.

What we are not promoting here is a maverick independence, devoid of any form of accountability and team. However, church leaders spend too much of their time rearranging the furniture – keeping things nicely ordered and stage-managed, trying to ensure that nothing ugly or misplaced happens which may make people feel uncomfortable or unduly disturbed! In this kind of environment, the prophetic, evangelistic and inspirational ministries are often either not recognised or most certainly alienated from any forum where they can have an authoritative role in genuinely influencing what goes on. The general consensus seems to be that while it is good to have inspiration and prophecy, let us not allow these to affect our foundations too much!

Mission and calling

Celtic missionaries had a deeply rooted theology of calling and for them its roots went right the way back to Abraham who was asked to go to a new land. They saw themselves as following in the footsteps of Jesus, for whom there was nowhere even to lay his head. Calling was extremely important. The highest call was to leave your country and comfort to serve Jesus, but as Columbanus' story shows, it was also an extremely noble call to desire to leave, but to choose to stay because of home duties.[2]

---

[2] See Appendix 1.

We believe that for too long mission has been separated from mainstream church life and the only people who have been available to take up the call have been the missionary societies or so-called parachurch organisations. Well, God bless them and long may they continue to do it! While everybody else has been standing around pontificating over the right way to do things they have got on with it. In generations past they have sown seeds in places like China, Korea and Argentina from which now, many generations later, we are seeing a considerable harvest.

However, we believe this sense of dynamic mission and calling needs to be right at the heart of church. Every Christian is a missionary, so therefore as part of normative church life we need to see people making decisions to go, and to invest themselves in different settings and people groups in order to see churches planted. Over the past fifteen years we have probably seen well over 100 people in our own church move house and relocate into different geographical locations in order to facilitate church-planting and other activities.

Recently, a couple of our key leaders, who are relatively newly married, have rented out their nice comfortable home in Chichester and have moved into a student flat in Southsea to work among students. Also, at the same time, they have planned to have their first child and to bring the baby up in an environment of radically serving God. Not for them the moving to a more comfortable and settled area of life because they are now having children. Far from it. They want to invest foundations for the future in their calling in God and have taken a move in the opposite direction to where most people would be going at this stage of their lives and marriage. We believe these kinds of decisions need to characterise the heart and life of many people at grass-roots in our churches. This is the only way we are going to come anywhere near an experience of what it is like to be on an adventure with Jesus, cutting ice in the society around us.

The inner journey

Celtic Christian spirituality presents our whole walk with God as a dynamic journey. Inwardly the process of repentance, resurrection and rebirth was perceived in these terms.

Scripture broadly gives us the sense that we have been saved, are being saved and will be saved. It is very important to know that we have arrived. We need to be aware of all that Jesus has achieved for us with his finished work on the cross and his dynamic resurrection. We have a vast inheritance. However, we believe that sometimes there is too strong a sense of arrival. In a way we *have* arrived, but this is only one side of the coin. We are still in the process of being saved and sanctified, and await the completeness that only heaven can provide. Sometimes both our thinking and understanding are too simplistic. Often our teaching degenerates into a type of 'ten steps to success' manual, which while having some benefit can in the end over-simplify things. We are telling people that we have all the answers, yet in the reality of their own lives they know that this is not the case.

If we can inspire them to see that their walk of repentance, change and sanctification in Christ is a dynamic adventure full of new horizons and indeed a little mystery, then they will be inspired to seek more. Those who will be apprehending God's kingdom will be those who have the greatest hunger and desire to seek. They will be the ones who feel the least able, the least qualified and who at the same time have a great faith in God's ability and desire to meet them where they are. They realise they don't have all the answers and that their walk with God is an ongoing adventure as they discover more of the boundless and fathomless love and wisdom of our Creator.

Passion

The dynamic Celtic missions came out of a deep love for Jesus and a phenomenal passion. Too often in the past expressions of tears, heart and emotion have been painfully lacking within the everyday experience of church life and in our corporate worship together. When Roger's wife, Margaret, was studying history at Cambridge she asked her non-Christian tutor for a comment on the attitude of the institutions and establishment within Christianity towards dynamic renewal movements. He said that in his experience the establishment stood for the squashing of excessive zeal and the maintenance of the status quo! Quite remarkable words, when coming from a non-Christian historian.

Patrick's passion for God is revealed in these remarkable words of commitment: 'Every day I am ready to be murdered, betrayed, enslaved – whatever may come my way. But I am not afraid of any of these things, because of the promises of heaven; for I have put myself in the hands of God Almighty.'

We are in a society that is motivated by gutsy compassion. The literal meaning of compassion is 'to suffer with'. One of the secrets of Princess Diana's popularity above other members of the Royal Family was her ability to engage passionately and compassionately with ordinary people. Too often in the church there is little humanity within our life and expression. Very few tears, very little

fire, very little virility and very little femininity in the way
we are operating. This seems at odds with Scripture. As
you look through the Psalms, the prophets and indeed
most of the New Testament there is no shortage of
passion and compassion.

One friend of ours wanted to challenge people with
God's dynamic character so he dyed his hair blond and
had the word 'fire' shaved at the back and dyed red! This
gave him numerous opportunities for discussion in the
pub with friends who weren't Christians and has caused
some provocation in the church he leads and further
afield in their city! Sometimes such symbolic acts are the
only way to confront people with the need for an awak-
ened, vibrant and passionate expression of faith.

The Celtic love for people, their enjoyment of art and
creativity, their engagement with culture and their
inspiration and deep submission to God are truly inspirational. At their best, they model an expression of faith
that is full of passion and conviction, yet at the same time
recognises our own poverty, brokenness and weakness in
the face of a wonderful, loving, heavenly Father.

Missionary journeys

As you read of the Celtic saints you will see that their missionary journeys were truly impressive. Brendan, it seems
likely, crossed the Atlantic in a coracle and therefore discovered America eight centuries before Christopher
Columbus! Columbanus travelled to France, Switzerland
and northern Italy, planting communities in places like
ruined temples of Diana! Others went to Austria,
Germany (where Boniface was later to have a profound
impact), Romania, Poland, Russia, the Faroes, and also
Iceland. It is interesting to note that the monastery where

Martin Luther first found faith was probably of Celtic origin.[3]

Cahill records the progress of the Christian Celtic missionaries across mainland Europe in the following terms: 'The white martyrs, clothed like druids in distinctive white wool robes, fanned out cheerfully across Europe, founding monasteries that would become the cities of Lumieges, Auxerre, Laon, Luxeil, Liege, Trier, Wurzburg, Regensburg, Rhienau, Reichenau, Salzburg, Vienna, Bobbio, Fiesole and Lucca to name but a few.'

The kinds of Christian communities they planted are a potential inspiration to us today. We are still only beginning to explore some of their challenges to our own thinking. However, we are sure that God wants to raise up key centres both in the UK and further afield that will become resource bases for mission in the same vein as Iona, Lindisfarne and indeed the Petrine and Pauline resource churches like Jerusalem, Antioch and Ephesus. As we encounter these expressions of church, our minds are expanded and broadened. These communities were extremely broad in their nature and make-up and inspire us towards big, flexible and experimental expressions of church. How we work out in more detail the issues of celibacy, community and the community of goods, education in the context of community and so many other areas is a matter for further thought and prayer. These are all part of the ongoing adventure.

In the missionary journeys of the Celtic Christians Jesus was the Alpha and Omega, the beginning and the end. For them Christ was the foundation. There is no point in going, risking or experimenting, being involved in any activity as Christians, if Jesus is not firmly in place

---

[3] See Appendix 1 for more brief biographies.

as our foundation. In that respect the structure of the communities enabled there to be discipleship and development so when people were sent out and released they came from a position of being approved and recommended by their community. The practice of having soul friends – people who were involved with them individually in areas of discipleship and shaping – meant that people could be meaningfully prepared, trained and empowered in the context of the community for their future calling in God.

Proper relational discipleship and development means that you don't have people wandering all over the place in a completely maverick fashion. In many situations people will do more harm than good in their efforts to bring Jesus to those outside of the church if they are poorly prepared.

The Celts' spirituality had a dynamic sense of constant movement. T. S. Eliot encapsulates their attitude: 'We shall not cease from exploration and the end of all our exploring will be to arrive where we started and to know the place for the first time.'

To be involved with Jesus is to be involved in life on the edge. The Celts lived in cold, harsh and wild environments. Their travelling by coracle often involved encounters with the power and dangers of the waves, encounters with large whales, icebergs, plagues and other frightening obstacles. Their exploration involved real risk.

If we are to go forward in Jesus we are not going to be able to avoid risk. However, these risks often bring us back to greater depths with Jesus. We become older, wiser and richer in his grace due to our adventures with him. As we learn from our mistakes we become more aware of his provision and totality, as well as of our own weakness and complete dependency on him. Although as mature

Christians we move away from the milk of the basics of the faith towards a more meaty walk with God, we never grow beyond his grace. In fact the further we go, the more we will marvel and be dwarfed and inspired by the incredible immensity of God's love and grace.

Too often our Christian life consists of being spoon-fed. Christians sometimes complain of impoverishment if they don't get their standard two hours' Bible teaching per week and a pastoral visit from the church leader. They probably have shelves full of different types of Bible, all sorts of tapes, resources and other forms of media at their disposal. Yet they wait to be spoon-fed. This is so far removed from places in the two-thirds world where the church is growing dynamically. Often they are sharing a Bible between large numbers of them and have no leaders to teach them because they are all in prison.

When people are cut free from these props they then have to find God for themselves and it is often groups under this sort of persecution that begin to experience the phenomenal grass-roots growth that characterises revival. We believe that if we are going to see this kind of phe-nomenon in our nation, the church is going to need to become more adventurous, experimental, flexible and dynamic. Come, Holy Spirit, and shake us upwards and outwards!

The Celtic pioneers had periods of incredibly intensive evangelism and activity, followed by periods of retreat and recharge in the wilderness, often for fifty days or more. Theirs was a rhythm of activity, action, silence and retreat. We believe there is an incredible inspiration and challenge in this. Many of us need to bring an increasing order and rhythm to our lives. The question from heaven is: Who is your Lord? Is it the career, the ministry, the calling, your family or Jesus Christ himself? The challenge for all of us is to have a rhythm that is in time with the right priorities. That means making adjustments.

In our own lives we have been trying hard to bear this in mind. We are building in rhythms of celebration, relationship and community. Rhythms of time with our wives and children. Rhythms of study, as well as rhythms of high-level exertion and effort in the context of our working activities. Some will need to make career decisions in this respect. People in our church have done everything from selling businesses in order to create a healthier rhythm, to embarking on job sharing with their partners within a restricted budget, to release more space. At times it will mean the acceptance of promotion and the reordering of life to achieve a healthy rhythm in the light of the increased commitment. In other settings it will mean the rejection of promotion in order to facilitate the wider areas of God's calling upon our lives in the broader areas of community. Everybody has a different adventure, yet all of our adventures should be shaped by the same principles of God's heart and kingdom.

The Holy Spirit, the Wild Goose

We know that there are some within Christianity who react to the term 'wild' or 'wild goose' in relation to the Holy Spirit. They are frightened by this classification, and to use the term 'wild' in relation to God seems inappropriate and even blasphemous to them. However, the word 'wild' in dictionary terms means 'untameable by human will, beyond human control, dynamic and exciting'. In these senses we would say that God is definitely wild!

In John 3:8 the Holy Spirit is likened to the wind, and in other passages throughout Scripture the word 'fire' is used in relation to the Holy Spirit. When a fire is blazing it is most definitely wild. These words are merely symbols and metaphors which communicate to us that the Lord God is beyond our control and will not be confined merely to our frameworks.

The Celtic term 'wild goose' is in a similar vein. It is said that when they saw the Barnacle Geese fly off together in their irresistible urge to migrate to other lands, Celtic Christians longed to take the good news of Jesus to those same places, often at great personal risk. They felt it was the Holy Spirit who gave them that longing to fly off and so they sometimes (though not always) called him the Wild Goose.

Although there is nowhere in Scripture where the Holy Spirit is called 'wild' or indeed 'the wild goose' it could also be said that there is nowhere either where the word 'Trinity' is named. There are numerous other universally accepted Christian terms, both in theology and church practice, that are either not used at all in the Bible or are not used in the same way that they are today – for example, church-planting, Reformed, Arminian, vicar, area superintendent, Evangelical, revival, awakening and renewal. Hopefully, however, these words are biblical in that they express the heart and meaning of a passage, a particular theological persuasion or a church practice, or they describe something seen in the Bible using contemporary words and images.

Symbols which have a rooting in their surrounding culture can, if they are consistent with biblical revelation, have an evocative and inspirational effect. Certainly the concept of the Holy Spirit as the Wild Goose encapsulates the sense of movement, adventure and dynamism which the Celtic pioneers expressed. The catching of this dynamic we believe will heal us of much of the sickness

and stagnation that is so often part of Western
Christianity. To the Celts nothing was static. Long before
anyone talked of quantum mechanics or relativity, the
Celtic Christians recognised the dynamic nature of
spirituality and creation. For them the analogy of the
Holy Spirit and the wild goose inspired them to go wherever the Spirit was leading. Certainly they had an incredible spirit of adventure. The Holy Spirit didn't have to
work hard to get them to engage in mission, even though
the costs were high. They packed up home and set off in
rudderless coracles at the mercy of the tides and currents.

Today we face many challenges. The Celtic dynamic will
inspire us towards exploration and adventure. This
will focus us in areas of vocation, creativity and gifting.
It will also give us energy to recapture a zest for life
which we may have lost within the predictability of our
everyday existence.

Furthermore, we must realise that the need to priorit-
ise and simplify our lives is right at the heart of retaining
this sense of adventure. Too often, the promptings of the
Holy Spirit are snuffed out by so-called sophistication and
other things which pollute the 'spiritual airways' of our
lives. New Agers talk much about 'centring our spiritual
energies'. Well, the only real and genuine 'centring'
involves human beings being refocused and founded
exclusively on Jesus Christ. In order to move forward
dynamically in the future, many of us will need to do an
audit of simplicity, both within our individual lives and
also corporately in the context of our churches. As we
have this simplicity and focus, then adventure becomes a
greater possibility. We have room to explore more of God
and move forward.

Sadly, however, for some leaders the concept of adventure is out of the question. Perhaps the current situation

or previous history restricts them to such a level that they have lost their ability to risk and lead dynamically into the future. Being in this situation is rather like being in a trap. Something needs to change and the Lord wants to open new doors in order to release people into their destiny.

Maybe their church has seen a measure of success and growth. They have moved away from the early days of insignificance and are now beginning to experience a measure of success. In that situation adventure ceases to be expedient. When we are nobodies and have nothing to lose, then risk and adventure are very much on the agenda. Subsequently, the onslaught of age and success brings change. Many are afraid to lose everything they have built, so they trade their sense of adventure and pioneering for the maintenance of all that has gone before.

This is always a sad scenario and in reality it is the next generation that will be sacrificed on the altar of safety, as they will eventually wake up and find they can no longer relate to the expressions and heart of the church they have been saved into and grown up through. For them the process of renewal and the cycle of adventure starts all over again, but with some casualties sadly destined to stay in the wilderness rather than coming into the new promised land that God will bring into being.

Colours of martyrdom

We believe God is challenging us as Christians to a greater level of adventure and pioneering. There will be a tremendous cost in that. Since Stephen, over half of all Christian martyrs died between 1900 and 1980 – over 26 million people. There have been over 9.9 million martyrs in the last forty years. There is a calling for us to move on. The challenge may not be to die for Jesus but it revolves around whether we are prepared to live for him. The Celts had a wonderful symbolism of colours. They talked of either red and green martyrdom or red, white and blue martyrdom. For them, red was the colour of blood martyrdom and enduring persecution for Christ. White martyrdom was the abandoning of everything for the love of God. Blue martyrdom was the freeing of yourself from evil desires by prayer, fasting and physically demanding forms of spiritual activity.

We believe God is raising up a generation that is prepared to adventure, to go and to be captivated with the mystery and excitement of serving God. They will be willing to take up the colours of red, white and blue martyrdom. Within this mix they will lay down their lives as witnesses (the Greek word for 'witness' being the root of 'martyr') – the word and life of the gospel embodied in lifestyle. The Celtic *peregrinati* (wanderers) are a challenge to us. They inspire us to a greater sense of adventure, freedom and creativity. We will only begin to be able to explore this through having our minds and wills radically challenged by God's truth, having our hearts and emotions fixed and stimulated by his purposes and having our spirituality enlivened by a richer and more holistic encounter with Jesus in our lifestyle.

9

A United Kingdom?

This book is our attempt to suggest a relevant application of the Celtic motif to the church in Britain and Ireland today. We wish to address one more issue which arises from the history of the Celtic church and which we believe has an ongoing impact upon us all. This aspect is perhaps less symbolic and more concrete, and flows directly from the historic roots described in Chapter 2. It is the issue of nationalism within the British Isles – especially in today's Celtic nations.

The authors are both English. We recognise this gives us a rather one-sided view. For this reason we have had this text read by friends in Ireland, Scotland and Wales. We are grateful for their insights and we hope that we have been able to deal with such a complex issue in a sensitive way.

Games without frontiers

The map of Europe has been seriously messed up over this past decade. When we were at school in the 1970s, the social and political balance had been stable for a generation. When we learned geography, there was simply East and West, NATO and the Warsaw Pact, capitalists and communists. All very predictable and certain. Without a Third World War it was hard to see how things could change.

Then one day a wall came down. It was a wall in Berlin that divided one nation by ideology. It was also a wall in people's minds that had said, 'Things will always be this way.'

As the last decade of our millennium opened, a fire began to spread across the continent. It is a fire of nationalism. National groups whose identity had been crushed by a succession of empires for a thousand years were seizing their day. Many of these groups were making demands that appeared to make little political or economic sense. For example, nobody suggested that either the Czechs or the Slovaks would be financially better off after the death of Czechoslovakia.

Then there was the insanity of the holocaust in former Yugoslavia, played out before a stunned world. In 1988 a group from our church smuggled some aid to Christians through the then closed borders of Romania. On their return, they spent some days in the beautiful historic Bosnian resort of Mostar. Five years later, Chris was literally dodging bullets in a very different Mostar – one now caught up in the violent hatred of Muslim versus Croat.

All this raises many questions as people try to understand the passion and power of nationalism. After 300 years of technological progress and rampant individualism, what were these destructive instincts gripping Europe? Why, all of a sudden, were people behaving in a medieval, even tribal, way towards their fellow creatures?

Whether a good or a bad thing, it seems that individualism does not have such a complete grip on our minds as we might have thought. People do have a sense of belonging. They want to express an identity that is greater than the sum of their personal relationships. If you like, there is a raw sense of tribalism in everyone.

Not that this tribalism need always be seen in ethnic terms. As we have shown, in a post-modern age of mix and match, this is the day of networking and mobility. For some people their tribe is a football club. For others it is an idealistic employer. However, the ethnic aspect is not one that can be ignored.

Nations under God

This leads us to something that is biblical and important on two levels. First, there is the consideration of the theological purpose of nations. Before going on, it is worth reminding ourselves that the Greek word *ethnos* originally meant 'a multitude' and later 'a nation or people'.[1] Throughout this chapter we will use the word 'nation' to describe what anthropologists call 'ethno-linguistic people groups', rather than political states.

The story begins with the cultural mandate of Genesis 1:26–28. God gives humanity the responsibility of filling the creation – in all its geographical diversity – with his image. As we know, the Fall spoiled this initial plan and soon after the Flood, nations were judged. In the Genesis 11 story of the Tower of Babel we see confusion brought upon them, but we should not see this as God utterly repudiating nations. As Paul said to the Athenians:

> From one man he made every nation of men, that they should inhabit the whole earth; and he determined the times set for them and the exact places where they should live. God did this so that men would seek him and perhaps reach out

---

[1] Vine's *Expository Dictionary*, p. 784.

for him and find him, though he is not far from each one of
us. 'For in him we live and move and have our being.' (Acts
17:26–28)

Paul suggests that there is something about people being
gathered in nations that causes them to look to God. This
perhaps explains why every pre-Christian culture has
types or shadows that can be filled to the full with
meaning when the gospel is preached. We mentioned
some of these in Chapter 1 from among the pre-Christian
Celts. There are other wonderful examples from around
the world.

One is found in the Chinese pictographic characters,
many of which are 3,000 or 4,000 years old. Thought to
be among the earliest is the character for the word 'righteousness'. This is composed of the symbol of a lamb over
the symbol of a man – an incredible sign that true righteousness would only come in humanity's justification
thanks to the Lamb of God. Another is an ancient pre-
missionary folklore tale of the African Lunda people en-
titled 'Who killed God's son?'.[2]

Just as nations have value in creation, so we are given a
glimpse of their importance in the age to come. John's
vision of heaven describes people of 'every nation, tribe,
people and language' (Rev 7:9). He also sees that the
glory of God fills New Jerusalem and 'the nations will
walk by its light, and the kings of the earth will bring their
splendour into it' (Rev 21:24).

Most fascinating of all we learn in the final vision that
through the centre of the city runs the river of life and on
each side of the river stands the tree of life: 'And the leaves
of the tree are for the healing of the nations' (Rev 22:2).

---

[2] The story is told in full in the late Gordon Suckling's *Kachongu Sesa-
Mbinga*, p.194.

Not only are there still nations in the renewed heavens and earth, but God is still healing them!

Here we touch on the difficult issue of how we understand the age to come. Clearly there will be both continuity and discontinuity with the present age. We believe that there is here a clear suggestion of an ongoing healing of nations in the age to come.

Holy nation

Second, thinking about nations points us to the 'holy nation' of God, the church (see 1 Peter 2:9). For us, joining church has been a healing from the emptiness of individualism. Twentieth-century technology – the car, the television, the personal computer, the superstore – means we need less and less personal contact with other people for our material survival and entertainment. Church is the antithesis to this lifestyle. We need to live open and vulnerable lives, sharing our deepest, darkest secrets and our loftiest dreams with others in our community of faith.

And here is where the two levels of nationality collide. Every person who becomes a Christian holds some national identity. That may be a very clear identity, or it may be very confused. Interestingly, the contemporary Celts of the British Isles – Welsh, Scots, Irish, Cornish – usually had a clearer sense of who they were than the English. We English usually don't feel very English ('I'm post-modern'), have more allegiance to our region ('I'm from Yorkshire'), or identify with a minority aspect of our identity ('My Granny's dad was Irish')!

Whatever we feel about our ethnic identity, on conversion we also acquire another, greater identity. That is, we become part of the completely international holy nation of God. Like our sex, our gifts and our tastes, our national identity does not become extinguished by our new Christian identity, but we must handle the former according to the latter. How do the two live side by side?

A ministry of reconciliation

To answer that question we can learn from another development of the 1990s. God is into signs. For example, physical healings are a sign that God's kingdom is close at hand. The person healed will inevitably die one day, but God's wisdom breaking in is a demonstration of his love and power. It is also prophetic of the future age where there will be no sin or death. Likewise, our actions against injustice and oppression are not with some naive goal of eliminating world poverty. And our creation-care work is not an attempt to 'save the planet'. These too are works that God will complete in the age to come. Rather, under the inspiration of God, we are seeking to prophesy about the coming kingdom.

One 'sign' that God appears to be highlighting in these days is to do with the prophecy we read in Revelation 22 concerning the healing of the nations. Again, we are not naive enough to expect that even a global revival can facilitate total world peace and harmony before the return of Jesus, but we want to take this sign seriously. Reconciliation has always been at the heart of the gospel. Indeed it is the summation of the gospel. There have been many profound blessings that have come from the emphasis on relationships in the church over the past few years. One of these has been to recover the truth that reconciliation is not just 'vertical' between humanity and God, but also 'horizontal' between people.

The cross of Calvary has both a horizontal and a verti-

cal axis. This is a symbol that Jesus' sacrificial death was
the most complete act of reconciliation in history. But his
life also wonderfully demonstrates reconciliation in action
from start to finish. He constantly worked to put people
right with God – the disabled man whose sins he forgave
before healing him (Lk 5:17–35); the woman caught in
adultery (Jn 8:1–11); Mary the former prostitute and
demoniac (Lk 8:2). He wanted to reach out, love and
clean up the lost and get them on the road again spiritually.

He also emphasised our need for right relationships
with one another – his teaching on judging and forgiving
in the Sermon on the Mount (Mt 6:9–15; 7:1–7); his
dealing with Martha and Mary's argument (Lk 10:38–
42) and James and John's competitiveness (Lk 9:46–50).
One of his greatest gospel parables concerns the healing
of a relationship between a father and his wayward son
(Lk 15:11–32). Most clearly of all, Jesus' lifestyle was
about constantly breaking the 'dividing walls of hostility',
as Paul called them in Ephesians 2, that split his society.
He addressed all these divisions radically. He valued
children (Lk 18:15–17); treated Samaritans with humanity (Lk 10:25–37; Jn 4:1–26); honoured women on
many occasions[3] and praised a Roman centurion (Mt
8:5–13).

Paul exhorts the people of Jesus to continue this ministry of reconciliation (2 Cor 5:18–21). Until fairly
recently the traditional evangelical view of this ministry
has been that it is restricted to the work of personal
evangelism. That is, to achieve reconciliation is to put

---

[3] See examples quoted above like the woman at the well, the woman
caught in adultery and Jesus' acceptance of Mary Magdalene's
support.

individuals right with God through conversion to Christ. The argument runs that if enough individuals get right with God, soon the whole of society will be sorted. This is an attractive idea but unrealistic. Personal evangelism is very much in Paul's mind in the context of 2 Corinthians 5 and is an essential part of the ministry of reconciliation. But there is more to it than that.

More recently, we have begun to see things from a wider perspective. We are beginning to understand that reconciliation is not simply about putting individual conflicts right. It is also about corporate and community issues. What's more, like so many other blessings of salvation, reconciliation does not come automatically with conversion.

Our scope must be wider than individualism. It must become corporate, and we must work at it together. As Paul famously said, 'Make every effort to keep the unity of the Spirit through the bond of peace' (Eph 4:3).

Peace – the health and wholeness of *shalom* – is a fruit of the kingdom of God, and the kingdom must be sought after (see Matthew 5:9 and Romans 14:17). Whether in our homes, our neighbourhoods or our nation, peace and reconciliation are things that we must pursue.

Healing the nations

When we see things on such a big canvas we can understand why nation-healing is high on the agenda. John Dawson's work on this subject has been most helpful to us.[4] He speaks of every nation having a 'redemptive gift'. In creation God intended that every nation should find

---

[4] Both *Taking Our Cities for God* and *Healing America's Wounds* are instructive.

God in their own space and make a unique godly culture. Through the redemptive work of Jesus – his sacrifice on our behalf – nations that turn to God have their own unique contribution to make to the world, to culture and to the worldwide body of Christ.

When we talk of a nation turning to God, we are not talking about the political state claiming to own Christian values, or even about the majority of the population turning to Christ in a revival situation. Rather, we are referring to the national (not state) church, whatever its size. That is to say, the church in the land defined as the sum total of all Christians. In some Muslim countries the church in any one *ethnos* might amount to only a handful. And we know that there are probably hundreds of *ethnoi* without this many believers!

However, before the nations can really bless one another with their redemptive gifts we must deal with the sins of the past. There is an obvious analogy with individual discipleship here. When a person comes to Christ they experience complete forgiveness and are set free from the power of sin. Then they are able to look forward to finding their role in the body of Christ. Unfortunately, normal experience dictates that wrong desires, bad habits and past blunders do not disappear overnight! They have to be dealt with. At this stage we feel powerless, unable to work things out alone and then we begin to learn to toil with the Holy Spirit who helps us to sort things through. Until we do this, although still loved by God, we will not be much use to him.

So it is with nations. Over the centuries there have been heinous atrocities committed by one nation against another. Some are recent and some are ancient. The ethnic/Christian mix really comes into play when we start seeing the church work across cultures. As individuals, we are able to be involved in the process of nation-healing as we respond to the Holy Spirit.

Many Christian people who are moving and working across cultures are finding that God is laying upon them a burden for the healing of nations. For others, it is not 'their thing', but if they are open to the Holy Spirit God will use them. We know of one woman who was speaking at a conference in Germany on church leadership. During one of her talks she suddenly became aware of the fact that here she was, a half-Jewess, speaking to a crowd of Germans! Full of emotion, she felt compelled by God to speak out words of forgiveness as a Jewish person towards sins committed against her people during the Nazi holocaust. The audience, for whom the guilt of history weighed heavy, were touched powerfully by God at this moment.

Ed Silvoso tells the story of how God used an Englishman, Roger Mitchell, to help to bring healing and a deeper move of the Holy Spirit into the revival context of Argentina. At an open-air mass rally in La Plata in 1993, Roger was invited to speak to the crowd. As he looked upon the sea of young faces, God touched him with the reality of some unfinished business between the UK and Argentina. He remembered that in one incident the lives of a thousand Argentine teenagers had been snuffed out during the Falklands/Malvinas conflict. This incident was the notorious sinking of the *Belgrano* battle-ship on 21 May 1982 while it was steaming away from the Falkland Islands/Malvinas and outside the exclusion zone. Without delving into the complexities of the diplomatic and political situation, Roger knew that he had to identify with that action and repent on behalf of the British and our imperialistic spirit. The response from the Argentine leaders was to be overjoyed and relieved: 'We have been waiting for years for God to send someone over who can say these things!' In time they too identified with their nation's sins in the conflict and extended forgiveness towards Roger.

These stories can sound rather superficial and naive. Who do we think we are, suggesting that we can deal with the wounds of the Nazi holocaust with a short word of forgiveness? Or the Falklands/Malvinas War with a quick 'sorry' and a prayer?!

The reality is that such wounds are not dealt with over-night, but that the process of humility, repentance and forgiveness can begin a work of nation-healing. If judgement begins at the house of God (see 1 Peter 4:17, RSV) then should it not be the people of God who take first responsibility for addressing these corporate sins? If the church cannot deal with the corporate sins of the past, who is going to do so? Surely we are not expecting politicians and diplomats to do the job!

It is not within the scope of this book to look more generally at the ministry of reconciliation. For further study we strongly recommend to you John Dawson's *Healing America's Wounds* (which is not just about America's wounds!).

Unblocking the well

Which finally brings us back to the Celts! Over these chapters we have drawn out many strands of what it means to be a New Celt: an adventurer for the gospel, passionate for God's life in all its forms, spiritual not worldly, sacrificial and yet full of celebration. These are characteristics that the best of Celtic Christianity revealed to us and lay into the spiritual foundations of these islands.

However, we are not claiming that reconciliation was one of these characteristics. During the zenith of Celtic

Christianity the Celtic peoples of the British Isles were clinging on to their last bastion of land before they were completely driven into the Atlantic Ocean. The Romans and Saxons pushed them further and further westwards and then the Vikings marauded them from every remaining coast. Perhaps with reason, the Celts were not so good at loving their neighbours. We have already shown that this gave justification to Pope Gregory for initiating his mission to the Anglo-Saxons in 596.

Instead, the subject of reconciliation is relevant because our desire to unblock the wells of Celtic Christianity reminds us of the ongoing tensions that still exist today between the Celts and the English. In Chapter 2 we left the story of the Celtic church at its point of conflict with Augustine's mission. The two defining moments in that conflict were first Augustine's meeting with the Welsh bishops in 602, then the Synod of Whitby in 664.

How important are these events in the current Celtic/English antagonism? Certainly there has been a running discord since that time. Could it be that a seventh-century spiritual rift of seismic proportions between the Roman church and the Celtic church has been causing reverberations for centuries? Surely it is not incredible that a church split on this scale could create a major stranglehold on the spiritual life of the church in these islands? If the destinies of ethnic nations are caught up with the progress of the church, then perhaps we should not be surprised by this. If we are correct, then it is down to the church to address it.

Two tribes

Chris has lived and worked in the Midlands and south-east England all his life. His ethnic pedigree is pretty straightforward working-class English (although his granny's mum is supposed to have been Irish!). Although he had been interested in his family's history, the business of his identity wasn't really something he had considered for the first twenty-five years of his life. It was only when Chris began to work with large events like Spring Harvest that the issue of national identity came to his attention. At Spring Harvest he found himself, on two or three occasions, working with or sharing accommodation with Scots people. These people were very friendly and pleasant generally, and yet he was aware of some strange unease that seemed to exist within some of those relationships.

On one occasion, Chris was speaking jokingly with his Scots room-mate in their salubrious Butlins chalet after the end of an evening celebration that they had both been leading. During the meeting there had been a bit of platform malarkey referring to England beating Scotland in a recent rugby match. Without really thinking, Chris said, 'You actually hate the English, don't you?' His roommate turned and looked Chris straight in the eye and without smiling said, 'Yes, we do.' After a few tense seconds the atmosphere broke and the laughter and good craich was soon resumed. But Chris did not forget that answer. He felt its depth and honesty.

Where did the Scotsman's strength of feeling come from? Did it come from a personal experience with somebody from England? Or did it come from a general sense of corporate mistreatment by a powerful neighbour? Later on, as Chris asked the questions, it became clear that it was the second answer that fitted. He was treated to a history lesson from the Middle Ages right down to the break-up of the Scottish steel industry and the introduction of the poll tax. Chris was informed how the Scots had been used as political pawns in Westminster's politics.

A degree of contempt for the English is unmistakable and seems to be lodged in the corporate psyche of many Scots. As Ewan McGregor's character in *Trainspotting* says, 'We couldn't even get conquered by a decent civilisation!'

Sunday, Bloody Sunday

The next stop in Chris's education was at the time of a March for Jesus in Northern Ireland. There he visited the front-line of the conflict, the so-called 'peace line' of West Belfast. The tension and anger there were tangible in the air, five years before the first IRA cease-fire. So was the anxiety of the driver who took Chris and his friend, Adam, up the Shankill and down the Falls. They were both in their twenties and with short hair-cuts they looked alarmingly like off-duty soldiers. They were given strict instructions not to open their mouths and reveal their accents if they were stopped!

The following year Chris returned with TIE Teams[5] to serve a Belfast church in an evangelistic outreach to a staunchly Loyalist working-class area of the city. Another education as they spent a week door-knocking tower blocks (as was the fashion then!) and learning how people felt about the English. This experience included speaking with an ex-convict who had 'carried out orders' (a euphemism for an execution) for the UVF. This time, he was convicted of his need for Jesus' forgiveness, but wrapped up tightly in the complexities of his identity, he held back.

During both these visits to Ireland Chris felt the

---

[5] A Pioneer evangelistic training initiative.

English (or, more accurately, 'the Brits') were seen with little respect from either side of the sectarian divide. To the Catholic/Nationalist/Republican community we represent the old oppressors. The history comes clattering down the years – the Norman invasions, Cromwell's atrocities, the brutal putting down of rebellions, abandonment in famine and the anathema of Partition. Right down to Bloody Sunday the pain is felt. To the Protestant/Loyalist/Unionist community the British represent a people to whom they have shown loyalty but who show them no commitment in return. Both these positions are extreme and could be argued against from history. But both positions come from real, strongly held perceptions and are rooted in truth.

During Chris's second visit he was told of a very informative vision that had been received by an Irish church leader, Davy Kidd, who has a recognised prophetic gift. He saw three characters: a brutal father, an abandoned mother and a bastard child. The father rapes the mother and the child is the outcome of the act of rape. The father then abandons the mother who escapes from his violence. The mother wants the child, but the child wants to be with its father. However, the father rejects the child, who is left feeling torn between its parents.

For the interpretation, read the father as Britain, the mother as Ireland (the Republic) and the child as Northern Ireland. This simple picture expresses the problem more eloquently than many words.

Wales and *Cymru*

With the Welsh, one of the most painful and divisive issues concerns their language. Chris has attended two meetings in Wales over recent years concerning the relationship between the gospel and the Welsh language. One was a meeting of evangelical academics and the other was a mixed gathering of charismatic and conservative Welsh intercessors. On both occasions he heard harrowing and heart-rending stories of the pain felt by individuals of different generations who had somehow suffered for their language or their national identity.

An older man had been beaten and ridiculed at school for having poor English because Welsh was spoken in his childhood home. A middle-aged woman had suffered disproportionate violence from police during protests for a bilingual Wales. Even a teenage girl told of how she was fed up with being teased at her English university for being Welsh. Chris found all this staggering.

On the other hand, there is pain from other parts of the Welsh nation. The re-emphasis on the Welsh language has had a negative effect on the English-speaking Welsh. Their culture and identity do not revolve around speaking Welsh. They don't particularly want to learn it, but at times they are made to feel like second-class Welsh citizens because they don't have Welsh.

Likewise, both the language barrier and the general Anglophobia that exists in some places means it can be hard for 'in-comers'. At one of these gatherings an Englishman who is a Church of Wales vicar literally broke down in tears when we started discussing this issue. He said that as an Anglican minister he had deliberately moved to Wales because he loved Welsh people and wanted to work among them in the gospel. He asked why he felt that all he had received in eight years was constant rejection from his Welsh fellow-believers.

If all this sounds rather far-fetched and emotive, why don't you talk to half a dozen Welsh, Irish or Scots people about it? Sure, you will find some who think that their compatriots are whiners and should drop the antagonism. They have no personal grudge, nor do they feel any pain in their hearts against the English. But there are many who do feel pain, both personally and somehow corporately. We could fill dozens of pages with stories to back up this contention.

Winners and losers

All this was quite a shock to Chris. He had been on holiday to Wales and Scotland many times, but this suffering was something he had never noticed before. This is probably a typical English – or rather a typical 'winner's' – reaction. As Chris has also found in Mostar and Johannesburg, it is the ones who have been pained who have the longer corporate memory.

When Chris visited South Africa for the third time in 1997 more than one white person told him, 'Apartheid is history now. We can forget it and start all over again.' His black friends told Chris that that is only a small part of the picture. For them, there is a need for justice. A need for apologies – not to mention restitution! The *raison d'être* for South Africa's Truth and Reconciliation Commission lies in its name. For there to be full reconciliation, first there must be truth. It is hard to forgive a wrong until that wrong is first identified and acknowledged. Then it can be faced. If there is repentance and apology, that helps the healing process no end.

During the war in Bosnia Chris talked with Croat people. They spoke about the cruel Ottoman (Muslim) rule over the Balkans as though they had experienced it personally. That empire crumbled after long and drawn-out death pangs in 1918. Talk to Serbian fighters and they would tell you of their hatred of the *ustachas* – the

Croatian Nazis who were allied with Hitler during World War Two. While the rest of Europe is planning for the next millennium in a spirit of unity and co-operation, these people are still reliving their painful, unresolved histories. The ruins of Vukovar testify to that.

The winner has the luxurious opportunity to forget the difficult things of history and move on. For the loser, history is still raw, recent and unresolved.

Identification

We should say at this point that we don't feel ashamed to be English. As we discover all the sins in our history there is pain and a measure of disillusionment, but there's no point in being 'whinging Poms' about our identity. There are many good things about our nation and about being English – for example, our sense of humour, our Dunkirk spirit when things are tough, our resourcefulness. What's more, this is who God has made us to be and as redeemed Englishmen we can do things that others can't. The opportunity to identify with corporate sins and to pray into historic wounds is just one example.

This identification is not an across-the-board thing, though. As English people, we can't just say 'sorry' to every Irish, Welsh or Scots person we bump into for our past sins. We're not advocating tokenism or melodramatic scenes for their own sake. These can become religious and unhelpful. But if history has caused us to come out as 'winners', then perhaps a little more sensitivity and humility towards our Celtic neighbours would go a long way. Perhaps a willingness to pray with them into these issues on occasion might do no harm, and yes, a willingness to say 'sorry' too. When we feel embarrassed as Christians about the religious nature of the conflict in

Northern Ireland, perhaps we ought to consider that we are a part of their problem – historically and currently.

Roman versus Celt

Before following this line of thought any further let us cut back to the roots of the conflict for the last time. We have sought to stress that in using the antitheses of Roman and Celtic we do not intend to be over-simplistic. It is clearly unhelpful to set up one to be seen as the incarnation of evil and the other as the incarnation of virtue. History is rarely so clean-cut.

However, again we would stress that the triumph of Rome over Lindisfarne was both deeply symbolic and also far more than symbolic. The historian Shirley Toulson argues that the Synod of Whitby was a more significant turning point in British history than the Battle of Hastings. She believes that at Whitby

> we lost a form of Christianity which, through its druidic roots, was truly linked to the perennial philosophy of humanity. . . . The leaders of the Celtic Church followed a religion that was primarily concerned with the relations between people, a religion of an isolated rural landscape, in which to meet a fellow human being is to hail him. At Whitby we traded that for a city-based religion, and in the cities people are amassed in crowds, to be manipulated, no matter how benevolently.[6]

The task of unblocking the Celtic well is first to recognise that our churches, like the Anglo-Saxons who first embraced Rome, have too often reflected the legalistic, imperial and safe options of the 'winners' of Whitby. It is

---

[6] Taken from her book *The Celtic Alternative*. Quoted from Bradley's *The Celtic Way*, p.25.

also to recognise that the spiritual pre-eminence of the English at Whitby, and the spirit in which it was won, foreshadowed our empire-building, both in these islands and beyond.

To unblock the ancient well, then, will mean that we need to repent when as leaders we have exercised a spirit of control in church life. It will mean that we must let go of people and allow them to be who they are. It means letting go of structures that do not serve the purposes of God today. It will mean repenting of using the church to fulfil our visions and our agendas.

Unity – the Holy Spirit's target

So what about the nations in these islands? We can't turn the clock back and undo fourteen hundred years of Roman/English domination over the Celts. We can't 'bring back' the Celtic church as was. So what *can* we do?

Graham Cooke is a man with a recognised prophetic gift who lives in Southampton. In 1991 he prophesied to Revelation Church about a number of things, including Chris being involved somehow in what he called 'a United Kingdom concept'. In his 1994 book, *Developing Your Prophetic Gifting*, Graham wrote about the word he had received back in the 1980s that began this thinking. This is part of that word:

> Unity is the great target of the Holy Spirit in the 1990s and beyond. We will see a move of God occur that will cut across all streams. As someone said, 'The day of the streams is over; the day of the river has begun.'
>
> We will see the demise of local, regional, national, and cultural barriers as the Lord begins a whole new process of unity and liberty.
>
> There will be a United Kingdom. I used to think the name

was a joke. However, in 1983 the Lord showed me it was a prophetic name. The Lord is raising up champions in the Celtic nations who will have a tremendous anointing for unity, who will turn the hearts of the nations towards each other. Lack of unity is a major stranglehold on revival.

We will have conferences and conventions, not just aimed at speaking for unity, but actively promoting reconciliation, apology and restoration. Forgiveness and healing will flow. The North/South divide in England will perish. Inter-county and inter-city rivalry will die. Lancashire will stop fighting the War of the Roses with Yorkshire. Cities will be twinned in heart and spirit. Liverpool will stop hating Manchester. This kind of rivalry is repeated throughout the nation.

In the realm of the Spirit, England must recognise that she needs her Celtic brothers. Repentance must flow, ancient hatreds must be laid down.

These conferences will be devoted to tearing down strong-holds of history, bigotry, treachery and betrayal. As these things are finally dealt with, we will see economic and spiritual revival breaking out in these areas.[7]

We quote Graham at some length because this prophecy summarises a number of the issues that need to be faced. They need to be taken seriously if we are to reclaim the ground that has been lost since the seventh century. In a few words, this message contains many of our feelings on the subject of a United Kingdom. In using the phrase 'United Kingdom', we understand Graham to be describing the experience of unity between the nations of these islands and the kingdom of God. It is not intended to have explicit political overtones. To conclude this chapter, let us look at a few phrases and point to ways in which we might move forward.

---

[7] Graham Cooke, *Developing Your Prophetic Gifting*, p. 36.

A demise of barriers

First we understand that boundaries are good but barriers are bad. The distinctiveness of the Celts and English is fine and God-given. As English people we should admire the Celts, appreciate them and honour them, without feeling that we have to deny our Englishness. To be a 'New Celt', as we are calling it, is to pick up the baton of Celtic spirituality. To walk as they walked with God, but in our culture.

The barrier between the Celtic nations and the English nations is surely a barrier to the working of the Holy Spirit. He will work wherever he chooses, but there is an undeniable link between the unity of believers and the 'anointing' of God's powerful presence. David, in his famous poem of unity, makes this comparison directly: 'How good and pleasant it is when brothers live together in unity! It is like precious oil poured on the head, running down on the beard, running down on Aaron's beard, down upon the collar of his robes. . . . For there the Lord bestows his blessing, even life for evermore' (Ps 133:1–3). The 'oil' in the psalm is the oil of Aaron's anointing for office. This is where God confirmed his authority and promised to be with him. Our anointing is with the 'oil' of the Holy Spirit to preach the good news and do the works of God. So where there is unity, there is more room for the Holy Spirit to move.

When we discussed the business of nations above, we mentioned that *ethnos* is about ethno-linguistic people groups, not political states. Thus, whether we look at the definition of 'nation' in terms of the UK and Ireland, or of 'these islands' as one entity, we have to conclude that there are several nations involved. Indeed, although we have used the term 'Celtic nations', it is important to recognise that there are several distinct Celtic nations within these islands. Ireland, Wales and Scotland all agree, but some would add Cornwall and Northern Ireland. These nations have their unique gifts and tensions to mix into the 'United Kingdom' pot.

The aim of the ministry of reconciliation and nation-healing is not simply to create some international 'kum-bah-ya' moment of harmony between all peoples. It is that we will be more equipped to fulfil the Great Commission. It is not going to be easy to 'make disciples of all nations' (Mt 28:19), especially the nations next door, if there are thumping boulders of hatred and resentment standing between us.

Where there are barriers, we must work to see these go. As we mentioned in an earlier chapter, the old divisions of denominations and streams are less relevant today than the networks and local expressions of unity that we see occurring. The Celtic/English barrier is a major blot on our spiritual landscape. Let us deal with it and move forward together!

Champions in the Celtic nations

It is interesting to observe that quite a number of people who have been banging the 'Celtic gong' over recent years have been English! We believe that this is a time for English people to move in the opposite spirit as far as the Celtic nations are concerned. Where we have taken we should be generous. Where we have withheld we should give freely.

We know of a number of the prophesied 'champions' referred to by Graham Cooke whom God is already raising up. We won't mention them, to save their blushes, but we believe that indeed this is a time when English and Celts could work together as never before.

God is still digging wells in the Celtic nations. Over St Patrick's Weekend 1997, Chris and a team from Revelation Church were invited to speak to a conference in Cork on the subject of Celtic Christianity. During the Saturday night celebration God prompted Chris to identify with the past sins of the English against the Irish, and to repent in some detail. What followed were remarkable experiences of the presence of the Holy Spirit which led to many finding emotional healing and the grace to forgive wounds that they didn't even know existed. Those present left convinced that God is doing something wonderful in drawing up from the ancient Christian roots of Ireland real water of renewal, healing and revival. Let's pray for our Celtic brothers and sisters. Not just the leaders, but every woman, man and child who gets a vision for these islands and beyond.

Conferences and conventions

Even in the past three years we have seen many tears and apologies and much healing and reconciliation. Nobody really seems to be organising it and there are doubtless many wonderful things happening that we don't know about. As was mentioned before, flowing with the Holy Spirit and avoiding hype and melodrama are of paramount importance. Sometimes events have been carefully planned, and others have been very spontaneous and chaotic!

One example of the first occurred in July 1996 near Cricklade, one of the suggested sites of Augustine's meetings with the Welsh bishops. This was not a formal occasion but involved drawing people together who felt we should pray into the historic roots of Celtic/English conflict. Some felt able to represent the Welsh bishops (that is, leaders from Wales), others the Roman church (that is, Catholics and Anglicans) and the rest joined in as they felt appropriate. Prayers of confession, repentance and forgiveness were said, and there was a simple sense of peace afterwards. The gathering was not long and not highly emotional, but everyone involved felt an obedient step had been taken towards healing a deep wound.

An example of the second would be during our first encounter with the current move of the Holy Spirit in 1994. During one of our 'refreshing meetings' as we called them, the issue of English/Celtic conflict somehow arose. In the middle of the suburban Sussex Riviera we spontaneously began praying and weeping for the sins of the English in Ireland, Wales and Scotland. Some dismiss these things as mere catharsis. We would point out that many who were touched at this and subsequent meetings continue to pray for revival in the Celtic nations.

One word of warning. We have already suggested that it is all too easy to become tokenistic and superficial when touching issues of reconciliation. On more than one occasion when Chris has spoken in Ireland he has been asked not to repent in public on behalf of the English. The second time this happened he asked why the leader did not wish this to happen. It was explained to Chris that a group from his church in Ireland had visited a well-known church in England for a conference. During this conference, a word came that the English should pray for the Irish. Everyone who was Irish was called out to the front of the meeting. For some reason the microphone was passed to someone who, while undoubtedly having a loving heart, unfortunately had insufficient sensitivity, faith or knowledge of what to pray for in this complex situation. All he could manage was, 'Lord, we repent of all we have done to the Irish. We're sorry for telling those racist Irish jokes.' And he wasn't joking this time! Apparently, the Irish did begin to weep, but their tears were not tears of healing. They were tears of pain that nobody even knew what had been done to them, apart from telling a few jokes!

Chris has tried to learn from this. When it has been appropriate to identify with the sins of the past, he has made sure that he knows what needs to be dealt with and he has spelled it out in the right amount of detail. It's back to the point raised in South Africa – not just reconciliation, but truth as well, to make that reconciliation real and lasting.

English repentance

Whether we like it or not, the English have a terrible reputation for being proud and arrogant. As rulers of the British Empire we gave off an imperious air that nobody was quite as good as us. Old habits die hard.

Once again, without doing a whitewash on history, we have to acknowledge the sins of our colonial past within these islands. The political concept of the 'United Kingdom' derives from the first serious colonial actions of the English – to dominate and to rule the 'Celtic fringes' of these islands. The Acts of Union and Acts of Settlement passed in the eighteenth and nineteenth centuries only brought to conclusion the centuries of creeping English ascendancy.

The Union Flag, combining the formerly separate colours of St Andrew, St George and St Patrick, was devised to demonstrate the blending of a true unity. In reality, it masked the English dominance won in military victories at Kinsale, Culloden, Aughrim and other places. Of course over the following years we carried this domination (mixed with blessings too) to every continent, as the British Empire spread.

If as church we are to be the agents of the healing of the wounds of this land we must be conscious of this. Shallow triumphalism must have no place among us. As English Christians we must be sensitive to the Holy Spirit and as such willing to yield, to apologise and to be generous.

Wider application

We want to stress that the principles we have outlined here are not only relevant to Britain and Ireland. Both the ministry of reconciliation and the priority given to aboriginal apostles are very much international themes at present.

We began this chapter by showing that nationalism has been one of the motifs of the 1990s. While nationalism has its down-sides, one of its positive features has been to highlight the plight of minority nationalities, many of them the 'host peoples' of a land. This has been particularly true in the New World – Native Americans in North and South America, Australian Aborigines, Maoris in New Zealand and so on. It is interesting to consider the Celtic/English conflict against this global background.

There has been a strong call for justice from organisations like Amnesty International, World Development Movement and Christian agencies such as CRED, to address the contemporary problems of oppression and human rights. This has been mirrored by a grass-roots response among Christians who have begun to grasp the damage done by the cultural imperialism which is implicit in the evangelistic approach of many Western missionaries. There have been pioneering acts of repentance, reconciliation and restitution undertaken, for example, by Dave Garrett in New Zealand, Wayne Drain in Arkansas and Ray McCauley in South Africa. Reconciliation is only through the cross of Christ, but action must often follow prayer. Such action has sometimes involved financial restitution. At other times there has been an encouragement to indigenous peoples to create worship songs and experiences that reflect their roots for the first time.

So there are wells to be unblocked all around the world. A renewed appreciation of indigenous cultures, a reconciliation between host peoples and immigrant peoples, addressing issues of justice and land rights – all reflect the New Celt ethos. History is always complex and fraught with danger in its interpretation. But these complexities should not stop us from facing the challenges of being not only a redeemed, but also a redeeming community.

Conclusion

Returning to the British Isles, we ask, 'Are there signs that things are changing?' Hopefully, the walls of division are cracking. The Scottish and Welsh assemblies are giving back some power from Westminster. The Northern Ireland peace process is underway, however slow and stumbling. Perhaps it is significant in the light of this chapter that one of the blueprint proposals for Northern Ireland involves a 'Council of the Isles'. Even Tony Blair got in on the repentance act and apologised shortly after his General Election victory for the actions of the Westminster Government during the Irish potato famine in the nineteenth century. At the time of writing there is talk of an apology for the Bloody Sunday massacre in Derry, and of a full enquiry being reopened.

These things are good and valuable, but the real problem lies deep-rooted in these islands. It is the church that should be taking a lead in the work of Celtic/English reconciliation. God does want to restore our heritage and unblock the ancient wells dug by our fathers. He does want us to pick up the baton to be the New Celts. But there is work to be done. There is praying to be done. There are relationships to be built. This is one of the many exciting challenges for the New Celts.

We finish with the modern telling of an old tale. Mel Gibson's *Braveheart* paints a colourful backdrop to close. The film was yet another portrayal of the sins of the conquering English. In contrast to this, the Holy Spirit Braveheart cry of 'Freedom!' is not merely a yearning for liberation from one nation's control of another. It is a desire for freedom from the ancient antagonisms that have held us all back. A cry for a United Kingdom under the greatest King of all.

Appendix 1
Who's Who in the Celtic Church

One of the most significant hallmarks of the Celtic church was the quality of its leadership. The 'who's who' that follows represents not only individual personal ministries, but also the influence that they carried. This is but a selection of the Celtic saints set out for our further inspiration. For those new to Celtic Christianity we hope that this procession whets your appetite for more study.

- **Aidan** (580–651) was the second monk from Iona deputised to evangelise the Northumbrians. After the failure of his predecessor, Aidan was far more successful in establishing the first significant foothold of Celtic Christianity in Anglo-Saxon territory on the island of Lindisfarne. A man known for his holiness, he was also responsible for the training of such leaders as Hilda, Chad and Cedd. Aidan became a beloved friend to King Oswald who gave him a horse from the royal stables to help in his itinerant evangelism. Much to the king's dismay Aidan, instinctively humble, gave the horse away to the first poor family he met and continued his ministry on foot.

- **Boisil** was the seventh-century Prior of Melrose Abbey, a foundation planted out of Lindisfarne. Bede recalls Boisil as being a man of true holiness and scholarship and as a mentor of the great Cuthbert. He also tells a touching story of how Boisil, dying of the plague, spent the last week of his life with Cuthbert deep in the Gospel of John. This was a source of inspiration to Cuthbert and comfort to Boisil as he eagerly anticipated his resurrection.

- **Boniface** (675–754), although an Anglo-Saxon, qualifies as a Celtic missionary because he adopted their method of wandering evangelism. Wynfrith of Crediton (Boniface was a nickname) originally hailed from a monastery in Wessex. In the words of Christopher Dawson, he was 'a man who had a deeper influence on the history of Europe than any Englishman who has ever lived'.[1] Like Columba and Columbanus before him, Boniface's evangelistic approach was often full-on and dramatic, destroying pagan temples, smashing idols and challenging pagan priests. He is a good example of the positive benefits of the confluence of the *peregrinatio* of the Celts with the order and organisation of Rome. He worked with purpose and energy throughout Germany under papal authority and was eventually martyred in Frisia.

- **Brendan** (486–577) was born and discipled in a Christian community at the height of Ireland's spiritual influence. He became Abbot of the important monastery of Clonfert, but he fell under the spirit of *peregrinatio* like so many of his compatriots. Setting off westwards in a flimsy coracle with twelve brothers, we

---

[1] Quoted in Neill, *A History of Christian Missions*, p. 64.

cannot know for sure whether or not he reached America over nine centuries before Christopher Columbus. He certainly reached Greenland, saw many wonders, returned to Ireland and lived to be over ninety. Surely nobody captures the Celtic spirit of adventure like this man.

- **Brigid** (*circa* 450–523) was an Irish woman shrouded in many legends, largely because she shared her name with a pagan Celtic goddess. When the Irish were converted, some of their worship of the goddess Brigid was translated as veneration to the Christian saint, Brigid. But the Christian woman did exist and founded a hugely influential mixed monastery at Kildare. She seems to have been a strong and determined personality, committed to fulfilling her destiny in God. One symbol of this is that Brigid lit a fire in the monastery, to be tended only by women, which stayed alight for a thousand years, until Henry VIII dissolved the monasteries.

- **Cadoc** was a fifth-century hermit who was instrumental in Illtyd's calling. Along with David, Illtyd and Mungo, he helped to build up Christian communities all over Wales in the late fifth and early sixth centuries. This period is regarded by some as the most formative in the entire history of Wales.[2]

- **Cathald** is known to us as a *peregrinati* of the seventh century who originated in Lismore. He followed in the wake of Columbanus in his wanderings around Europe and finally became a bishop in Taranto in southern Italy.

---

[2] David Marshall, *The Celtic Connection*, p. 24.

- **Cedd** left the security of Lindisfarne in the mid-seventh century to become the evangelist to Essex man! He established a monastery at Bradwell-on-Sea, where the isolated St Peter's Chapel can still be visited in its wild coastal surroundings.

- **Chad** was reportedly the brother of Cedd. Like his brother he did not love his own life too much to keep himself from taking the gospel to the Saxons. He is attributed with converting the Kingdom of Mercia, basing himself in Lichfield where he died in 672.

- **Columba** is described by some as the greatest of the Celtic saints. Pioneer, politician and pious saint, Columba's voyage to Iona was a landmark unequalled in the brief ascendancy of the Celtic church. Adamnan's *Life of Columba* is full of confrontations with magicians over dead bodies, contaminated wells and even a chase with a mysterious monster in Loch Ness!

- **Columbanus** (540–615) was an Irish monk, and another of the Celtic greats. He was even stricter on himself and on his monks than his mentor, Columba, and he long held a desire to convert the distant Slavs. However, in a vision an angel told him that the whole world was a wilderness in which he could pursue his spiritual labours, so he stayed put on Iona for many years. His missionary journeys began when he was about fifty-five and they took him to Brittany, Burgundy, the Vosges, Switzerland, and eventually to Milan. Columbanus established an influential monastery at Bobbio that was certainly visited by Francis of Assisi. Perhaps it was from the Celtic stream that Francis imbibed his biblical love of nature.

- **Comgall** was a pioneer of the sixth century, establishing the important monastery at Bangor in Ulster. He probably discipled Columbanus and is credited with the saying, 'A man without a soul friend is like a body without a head.'

- **Cuthbert** (634–687) was one of the best-loved and most heroic figures of the period. He started life in the Cheviot Hills of Northumbria and became Bishop of Lindisfarne, but at heart he was an evangelist. As Bede notes:

  > He was wont to resort most commonly unto those places and preach in those hamlets lying afar off in steep and craggy hills, which other men had dreaded to visit, and which from their poverty as well as uplandish rudeness teachers shunned to approach; tarrying in the hilly part, he would call the poor folk of the country to heavenly things with the word of preaching as well as work of virtuous example.[3]

  Cuthbert was one of the saints whose intimacy with creation was recorded. In his case this included being fed by ravens and eagles, and during a night-long prayer vigil in the North Sea his feet were warmed by sea otters. Again he is renowned for the miraculous signs that accompanied his preaching.

- **David** (*circa* 500–589) was nicknamed 'waterman'. This was either because he was teetotal or because of his habit of quoting the Psalms up to his waist in the Irish Sea off the west coast of Wales! Born in Wales or perhaps Ireland, he was discipled at Ninian's *Candida Casa* and built on the foundations of Illtyd in developing the church in Wales. He founded the hugely influential monastery in the city that now bears his

---

[3] Bede, *History IV:27*.

name, which became an educational, spiritual and mission-sending centre for Wales and the west of England. In spite of this, David's influence on Welsh Christianity was more as an example of devotion and discipline than as a missionary leader.

- **Dicul** was the seventh-century Irish evangelist who was the first person known to take the gospel to the South Saxons. While the romanised Celt, Wilfrid, gets remembered locally, Dicul probably established a monastery at Bosham before Wilfrid was born.

- **Erigena (John Scotus)** appears late in the story of the Celts, being born in Ireland early in the ninth century. However, he is worthy of mention because like Pelagius before him he was a true Celt, a great theologian and he too fell foul of Rome! In contrast to Augustine of Hippo, he held fast to the essential goodness of creation, claiming that the natural destiny of all creation, including humanity, was to reach God through Christ. Erigena had many wonderful theological ideas. For example, he held that every object was a flash of the supernatural – God was more than Creator; he was the essence of all things. At the Synod of Valence in 855 Erigena was found guilty of heresy for arguing that it was logically and morally wrong to claim that God predestined some people to damnation.

- **Gall** or **Gallus** was a disciple of Columbanus, who became the apostle of north-eastern Switzerland. He founded a monastery at St Gallen that remained a vital well of Christian life and culture throughout the early Middle Ages.

- **Gildas** is best remembered as a prophet and as the chronicler of the Celtic church in Wales. He was born in Strathclyde, discipled by Illtyd, travelled to Ireland and lived in solitude on an island in the Bristol Channel for many years. He spent the latter part of his life in Brittany, where he founded a monastery at Rhuys. His classic work, *The Ruin of Britain*, is about the lukewarmness of the ancient British church and the Saxon invasions.

- **Gwinear** sailed from Ireland, evangelised in Cornwall and became a martyr.

- The two **Hewalds**, who were tortured and killed in Old Saxony before they had opened their mouths, were examples of great post-Whitby evangelists.

- **Hilda** was remarkable as a woman leader of a mixed monastery. We can all draw our own conclusions from the evidence of this leadership practice (borne out by that of Brigid in Kildare and Ita in Limerick), but clearly it has significant theological and ecclesiological implications.

- **Illtyd** (*circa* 425–505) was effectively the founder of the Welsh church. He was of noble Druid descent and an accomplished warrior at the time of his conversion. Seeking the life of a hermit, others followed him, and the monastic school at Llanilltud Fawr was established. In this time this school saw the education of such men as David and Gildas.

- **Issui** was a Welsh hermit who lived in the Black Mountains. He was martyred and the place of his hermitage became known as a sacred place of healing. When a merchant suffering from leprosy visited the site and was instantly healed, he left a bag of gold there in gratitude to God for his healing. The local people used this money to build themselves a church building. Patricio Church, somehow overlooked during the architectural vandalism of the Reformation, can still be visited in its breath-taking location.

- **Mawgan** came from Wales early in the sixth century. He was a disciple of Patrick and preached in Brittany and Cornwall.

- **Mungo** (518–603), also known as Kentigern, was appointed Bishop of Cumbria in 543. After persecution he fled to Wales, where he chilled out with David for a while. Returning to Scotland, his journeys stretched from Galloway to the Orkneys. The survival of Christianity among the Celtic peoples on the fringes of Britain owes much to people like Mungo. Details of his life are few, but his tireless pastoral and evangelistic efforts strengthened numerous churches and monastic settlements, preparing them to take the gospel further to unreached areas.

- **Ninian** was an early British Christian Celt, probably from north of Hadrian's Wall, who was trained in Rome. His significance lies in the fact that he was the first known Celtic Christian pioneer. He founded a monastery, the *Candida Casa*, in Whithorn in 398, which became an important missionary centre. Ninian is attributed by some to have evangelised much of Scotland, reaching the southern and the northern Picts. Among Ninian's disciples was Serf, who later evangelised Fife.

- **Patrick** (340–461) is probably one of the greatest apostolic figures in church history. A brief biographical sketch is to be found in Chapter 1. He was a man of piety and prayer whose thirty years of evangelism left behind thousands of baptised believers. But it was his ability to leave behind hundreds and hundreds of Christian communities that really marks him out.

- **Pelagius** (350–418) was arguably the greatest theologian of Celtic Christianity and yet history has dealt him a bad press. We know he was born somewhere in these islands, but he spent much of his life in Rome and died in Egypt. While in Rome he came into sharp conflict with the papacy and particularly with one of its greatest thinkers, Augustine of Hippo. The conflict arose over two of Augustine's key doctrinal contributions: that of original sin and predestination. Pelagius' view almost certainly represented early church orthodoxy until that time. Nobody articulated the Celtic values of creation and goodness of nature, or of freewill, as effectively as Pelagius. But in the debate, Pelagius was defeated and excommunicated. A classic case of history belonging to the winners, only Augustine's attacks on Pelagius' major works have survived. The author's originals have perished, so we will never know for sure whether his accusers' claims were true.

- **Piran** (fifth century), patron saint of Cornwall (which was said to be the last stronghold of the Celts), was based at a monastery near Tintagel. He is remembered as a friend of tin miners who also travelled to South Wales and Brittany. One author estimates that there were ninety-eight monastic foundations in Cornwall during the Celtic period.

- **Serf** was a disciple of Ninian and, as mentioned above, became an evangelist in Fife and a mentor to Mungo (Kentigern). He went on to found a monastery at

Culross. However, we mention him here because we love the fact that he had a pet robin. Better still, one hagiographer claimed that he discipled a lamb into the signs and wonders ministry. This ministry reached a peak when it saw a dead pig raised to life![4]

- **Wilfrid** (633–709), a contemporary of Cuthbert, was a complex character. Both men were involved in the momentous Synod of Whitby (663–664), which clearly marks a watershed with regard to the Celtic church. Wilfrid was born of an aristocratic Northumbrian family and spent much of his youth at Lindisfarne, serving a nobleman who had become a monk there. However, he spent many years on the continent where he adopted a number of Roman distinctives, including their calculation of Easter. He thus represents something of a symbol of the synthesis of Celtic and Roman Christianity in Britain – the engulfing but not necessarily the elimination of the former by the latter. After his exile from Northumbria in 680 Wilfrid was involved in pioneering evangelism which reached Sussex. Although not completely virgin territory, this was a last bastion of paganism in England.

- **Willibrond** (658–739) and **Wigbert**, who evangelised Holland and Belgium, are further examples of Celtic missionaries who followed the Synod of Whitby.

Who knows how many more names we will come to know in glory, when we all rejoice together at the grace God gave to these brothers and sisters!

---

[4] If you don't believe us ask Ian Bradley! Bradley, *The Celtic Way*, p. 55.

Appendix 2

Contemporary Case Study: Revelation Church

On a pilgrimage

We owe a great debt to the men and women who found themselves gripped by the rugged and rich spirituality of the Celtic church long before we were. Their writings, their research and their insights have significantly informed our study and reflection upon the Celts. We have also been challenged by some of the attempts that have been made to capture the spirit of Celtic spirituality in liturgies and lifestyles, particularly those that redress the balance of our busy age.

In these last pages we want to set out some of the ways in which we are seeking to flesh out what we understand by the 'New Celt' motif in our church. The comments are brief, aiming to give an overview of where we have got to. We offer these attempts to work out our ideas practically and with humility, recognising that they are incomplete and that we are ourselves on a sort of *peregrinatio*. We are journeying after God, often with a sense of frustration at the issues that remain unresolved, but trying to be faithful to what we have seen.

What we offer here is in no way definitive. We are not setting out our model against anybody else's. Some of the values we are expressing pre-date our appreciation of Celtic Christianity. We make reference to them here because we can see how they fit into a 'New Celt' grid.

Brief background

Revelation is a house church founded in 1983 by Roger Ellis and a group of twenty-five other teens and twenties. Like so many others, it was therefore a 'youth church' before that phrase entered our common Christian vocabulary. Always with a strong charismatic emphasis, Revelation Church became part of the young Pioneer network in the early 1980s, thanks to Roger's friendship with Gerald Coates. Without going into the details of our history, between 1986 and 1996 a church-planting programme was undertaken. This means that at the time of writing we are geographically spread along the south coast from Bognor Regis in the east, through Chichester and across to Portsmouth in the west. In addition to planting in a couple of villages in between, we have also released those under twenty-five to express church within youth and student culture under the title of 'Warehouse'. There are Warehouse cells in Bognor Regis and Chichester and among the student communities of Southsea.

The ways in which we are seeking to embrace Celtic values will be examined under the headings of community, leadership, church, creativity, spirituality and discipleship.

Community

The Celtic church created a healthy balance between community and solitude. The monastic foundations established by Patrick, Columba, David and Aidan all had an emphasis on deeply personal devotion that was often expressed through hermitage. They also developed as discipling communities. But they were in the world – preaching to surrounding villagers, feeding the poor, offering hospitality.

We have always appreciated the concept of community. Having grown up with Gerald Coates' teaching on church and relationships we have sought to foster a sense of the church as a loving community. Alongside this we have also wanted to stress that the church must be part of its wider community – city, town, village.

Recently we have been greatly helped by the teaching on cell church by Ralph Neighbour and William Beckham. The concepts of minimalism, empowerment and responsibility struck a chord as we were looking at the Celts. So we have begun to restructure Revelation Church in its most radical shift since we began church-planting twelve years ago. We have deconstructed our congregations, and our congregational leaders (local elders) have all voluntarily stepped down. In their place there is now one area leadership team overseeing all of our cell groups. In place of the congregations we are restructuring the church into small cell groups of about ten people. The cells are peer groups covering a broad age range – from seven-year-olds to senior citizens – to enable them to form relationships and reach their peers more effectively. Although we previously had house groups, these groups look very different, with a deeper level of mutual interdependence and a stronger degree of evangelistic emphasis.

We are going for a model of unity and diversity. At the time of writing we are at a very early stage in the process, but we currently have around fifty cells of different shapes and sizes. At present these cells cluster together three out of four Sundays, either based on their geography (Chichester, Bognor Regis, Portsmouth, Selsey) or demography (Warehouse – youth and students). Once a month we celebrate at a central gathering of all our cells. The cells represent different 'tribal' groups, but we are all part of the one 'nation' that is Revelation Church.

Within our lifestyles we have sought to break down the individualism of our society that is often expressed in the nuclear family. Many households have experimented with the concept of the extended family to differing degrees. In some situations single people live with married people. This arrangement can be beneficial at a number of levels. One of the most radical models has been where a child-less married couple have joined household with a divorced mother and her child on a long-term basis.

Among the single people in our church there have also been expressions of extended households. Some of these have involved single-sex households and some mixed households – like the Celtic houses, both are celibate of course! Again, one of the more radical experiments involved two single girls who took in a solo mother and her six-year-old daughter for a year.

The keynote we aim for is flexibility. Some keep a room for hospitality. For families and singles alike there are seasons that change. We want to encourage people to capture these seasons without being enslaved to the god-less treadmill of self-improvement and self-enrichment.

Having said this about economics, we are still a long way from the Acts 2 values of community of goods and the Celtic virtues of simplicity. Our church still reflects fairly standard middle-class concerns and tastes when it comes to living standards. Many people give sac-rificially both to the church and to other good causes, but others do not. We have some journeying to do on this one!

Church in community

In 1991 a group of us, under the inspiration of Mike Morris, began to look more keenly at the Scriptures. We were looking at the question of how as church we should be responding to our role in society. Under the banner of 'Christian Citizenship' we then sought to educate the church on our inherent responsibilities to the community around us. Now styled under the title of Revelation Community Development, we have learned many lessons, but generally we have gained a positive reputation in our communities for delivering what we promised. A summary of our current activities is as follows:

- **Sign language** courses run every week, with new courses being planned for the future. A number of deaf people have now joined the church.

- **Overcomers** is a weekly group for people from inside and outside the church who are trying to take control of an addiction or life-controlling problem. This is linked to the organisation Bridges International, and new people coming into this would also be in a cell group. Someone in their cell would be alongside them, and that person would have the option of attending the group with them in order to maintain a relational link into the wider church.

- Our **visiting programme** involves volunteers visiting lonely, often elderly, people in their homes for 'tea and chat'. This happens in Chichester on an irregular basis.

- Members of our Bognor Regis cells run an **Evening Care Respite Scheme** in a Social Services day centre, for people with disabilities. This happens on a monthly basis. Clients are collected in the day centre's minibus (for which volunteers have passed a special driving test) and volunteers' cars, and brought to the centre. The volunteers arrange an evening of entertainment and then take clients home. Currently there are twenty-six clients on the books, but we cannot take any more due to a lack of extra drivers.

- Members of our Chichester cells donate food once a month to the **Chichester Food Boxes Scheme**. This is then sorted out and delivered to households in the city that have given consent and have been referred through their social worker. This scheme has been approved by Social Services. Currently we deliver to six households.

- We also have a **referral system** whereby requests for help come into the church office and are then passed on to the local co-ordinators who find people to carry out the jobs. This is currently being reviewed and we are thinking of changing the name to Revelation Community Volunteers or the Revelation Volunteer Scheme.

- The **Revelation allotment** is rented from Chichester District Council to provide purposeful activity for unemployed members of the community who grow fruit and vegetables to be used for the Food Boxes Scheme and St Joseph's – a local night refuge for homeless people.

- **Playschemes** have been run over a number of years in Chichester, Bognor Regis, Portsmouth and Barnham and serve 80 to 120 children for a week in each place. We have catered for a number of children in Bognor

Regis and Chichester playschemes who have had special needs. We would like to develop the community aspect of this further in 1998 and have just received a grant from the Variety Club to buy equipment for children with disabilities to use at next year's playschemes!

- The **Parenting Skills Course** is an eight-week course run for people inside and outside the church to help parents improve skills and share difficulties. Using an internationally recognised course, this has provided great opportunities for sharing the gospel.

- Over the years we have carried out **green audits/creation care audits** in individual households and also for Christian organisations. We are looking to get our cells doing this themselves as part of their lifestyle. Chris and a team from Revelation undertook a major green audit of Tear Fund in 1996. This has led to the production of their comprehensive environmental policy.

- A **carers group** is currently being researched and initiated in Selsey.

- A **domestic violence forum** is currently being researched following a request by a secular solicitor in family law, to see what the needs are and how we might be able to respond. We want to go very slowly with this to ensure we don't make damaging mistakes. We will liaise with our trained counsellors and possibly have this as a target for those who want to be involved in the community.

- **Community development consultation days** draw together a number of people across the church to support, share and encourage our community involvement. These days also provide a forum to network across the church.

- A representative is involved in our **Building Working Group** to ensure that Revelation considers access, environmental issues and community use of our building resources.

- We are currently looking at a **shop front** on a local housing estate, run by Revelation in partnership with the local community. This would provide an information point on the estate.

In addition to these initiatives, Revelation also supports the following community activities through the Community Development Programme:

- **All Sports Club** – for adults with learning difficulties. This is run at the youth wing in Chichester.

- **Pregnancy Advice Centres** – Bridge Pregnancy Crisis Centre in Bognor Regis and Options Pregnancy Advice Centre in Chichester are both inter-church and affiliated to Care for Life.

- **Bognor Community Furniture Services** – run by volunteers mainly from Revelation.

- **Chichester Christian Care** – day centre and St Joseph's night refuge for homeless people. We are continuing to pursue a supportive role with this inter-church project.

- **Local Residents' Associations**

- **Victim Support** – national organisation helping victims of crime and accident. People from our Bognor Regis cells are involved with this initiative.

- **Floral Pride Group** – we have been involved with a planting programme (flowers not churches!) with Chichester District Council over the last few years and intend to continue this into the future.

Justice

In a day of global politics and economics, we have also sought to take the issues of justice on board as a church. We have supported the work of Christian Aid through local Churches Together. We have also been involved with campaigns for religious liberty co-ordinated by Mike Morris while he was at the international desk of the Evangelical Alliance.

More recently, Greg Valerio has pioneered the work of CRED, which operates from our Chichester office. Back in 1991 Revelation Church began a development education programme in local secondary schools.[1] Our brief was to talk to and educate young adults about the world in which we live. In order to add authenticity to the equation a trip to Tanzania was undertaken. Following on from this we learned that investment into the issue of justice required our rediscovery of the God of justice. CRED was born in September 1994.

Following a trip to Ethiopia in 1994, an International Education Fund was started and a limited company was set up to meet the felt needs of education and employment in the urban slums.

CRED continues to grow and other churches are attracted to the noise we are making concerning justice for the poor. A Bristol office has now been opened in partnership with Bristol Christian Fellowship. We also

---

[1] A resource pack, priced £5.95 + postage and packing is available from CRED, PO Box 58, Chichester, West Sussex PO19 2UD.

have a partnership arrangement with And Albert Plc. This national chain of Fair Trade shops makes economic justice for the poor work at the high street.

In response to the many individual enquiries we have received, CRED has now been launched as a membership organisation/network.[2] This has added the icing to the cake and has attracted the attention of Katharine Hamnett among other household names.

Painful world

Whenever we get caught up working with the pain in the world it presents challenges and paradoxes to a simplistic spirituality. We rejoice in the evidences of the God of the supernatural breaking in all around us. However, we are also deeply affected by those who have not been healed. Perhaps this is a touchstone of having a holistic worldview. Can we hold together the celebration of life with the mourning at the pain of the Fall? The harshness of Celtic monastic life married to the love of creation was one of the ways they recognised this paradox and tried to reconcile it. We are having to re-examine our theology a little in order to do the same.

Leadership

By 1996 we had reached about 600 church members in five congregations. Our structure had created a context where as leaders we faced the danger of becoming increasingly detached from the grass-roots of the church. Many members of the leadership were (and still are) involved in national ministry to some degree or other. In addition to this, as a

---

[2] Contact Greg Valerio at CRED, PO Box 58, Chichester, West Sussex PO19 2UD.

community, we have always excelled in projects. We came to see that in all the projects and activity we were losing something vital in the realm of 'being' as against 'doing'.

When we looked at the Celts we started to see that a new rhythm for leadership was required. The abbots, abbesses and priors were strong and uncompromising – some might say dictatorial – in their leadership, but they lived with their communities. We wanted to avoid becoming bureaucratic and 'top down'. Our model was not to be taken from the business world but from Jesus, the Twelve and the church in Acts.

Cell church has enabled us to begin to address these challenges. We have drastically trimmed our church diary. We don't want to turn the lives of church members into an unending treadmill of meetings and teams. As we said, we have deconstructed, reformed and simplified our concept of local elders, cutting back on a whole tier of leadership.

Every leader is in a cell, whether or not they lead one. We are encouraging one another to share openly in that cell and to make attendance at it a priority. We see this development as crucial to redefining the concept of leadership. We are rejecting the Western idea of a pope or 'God's person of power for the hour'. Instead we are trying to recover the more Eastern idea of learning together with leaders facilitating – the teacher showing as well as telling.

Within this there is a clear feeling of risk, adventure and personal growth. There is plenty to lose, but we feel that the price tags have been changed. We are valuing things differently from how they were valued three years ago.

Church

Considering the transport technology available to the Celtic Christians, their experience of church was remarkably global. Patrick famously said, 'The world is my parish,' and the exploits of so many names show that they acknowledged few boundaries in their commitment to follow God.

Someone has observed that the word 'local' appears to be a canonised prefix to the word 'church' in the West. Perhaps this is a point that can be made from the Celtic/Roman split. The Anglo-Saxon's eager adoption of Augustine's parochial system meant that the concept of church quickly became solidified until today, when most of the population use the term to mean a building rather than a community.

In contrast we can look at Iona and Lindisfarne as centres whose life spread across these islands and right into Europe. These in turn remind us of some of the New Testament counterparts of such places: Antioch, Corinth and Ephesus. In both cases there was clearly a measure of accountability to a localised base, but also a strong drive to 'go' into the nations.

In Revelation Church we have been exploring the concept of 'church' and 'movement' over the past few years. That is, we have begun to recognise that the work of the Holy Spirit among us has facilitated a grass-roots expression of church which has extended and overlapped into many local, national and international projects and relationships.

While there is an ongoing mutuality and interdependence between the local and wider ministries, we have sought to define the local in terms of the 'church' and the wider in terms of the 'movement'. The life of the community depends on the wider vision and thrust of the movement, while the resourcing of the movement depends on the strength and depth of the local community.

Bringing a slight distinction between the two aspects enables us to ensure that both are appropriately resourced and cared for and that together we are released to maximise our potential. Added to this, we are a part of Pioneer, a national network that provides valued input and apostolic oversight to us. Some aspects of the vision that has come from Revelation Church have been broader than local church. Many of these have been fleshed out in partnership with Pioneer and have become part of its wider vision. For example, Equipped to Lead, DNA (formerly TIE Teams) and other leadership initiatives.

On the other hand, there have been aspects of our vision that have not been expressed structurally through Pioneer, but have been worked out through different relationships. We have served alongside others and have had some role in facilitating things like Fusion (the national student initiative), Remix (catalysing the planting of churches into youth culture) and CRED. Furthermore we have provided a relational base of love, care and accountability from which some key individual ministries have been able to operate.

Just as the Celtic knot turns and weaves, so our lives and relationships rarely run in straight lines. Instead they are more like prophetic 'wheels within wheels'. Breaking our minds free from a hierarchical and linear approach to leadership and church will have implications on a number of levels.

First, internally, it means that the life of the church should revolve less around the leaders. We are working to encourage people to pursue their Christian calling in the work place. For too long the hierarchy of callings that sees 'full-time Christian work' as the pinnacle of spiritual success has held us back from effectiveness in the community. The best evangelistic initiatives, the most prophetic actions, the greatest works of love are less likely to be in our meetings than in the local school, on the building site or in the office block. So we are looking to encourage people to see their calling in a broader context.

Second, in our relationship to the rest of the body of Christ we recognise that God is calling us to be a movement within a movement. We are grateful to be part of Pioneer as an organic network of relationships. We gladly make ourselves accountable to Gerald Coates, Steve Clifford and Alistair Bullen, whom we acknowledge to have an apostolic role in Revelation (church and movement). As a leadership team we regularly meet with these friends and work through major decisions with them. We owe a lot to them personally. But we recognise that our identity is within a broader context than merely Pioneer. These are wheels within wheels. There are other churches within our region that happen to be Pioneer churches and we work and have close relationships with them. We are also committed to working with other churches in our towns and cities that might have a totally different flavour.

Third, there is an international dimension. Just as the Celtic stream flowed into Europe through Columbanus at Bobbio and elsewhere, so we are committed to seeing our stream flow over frontiers. During recent years we have been challenged to look more seriously at our international involvement. We have released workers who know God's calling to work on a short-term or medium-term basis into Albania, China and South Africa. More recently we have been approached by groups in New York, Germany and Zambia that are looking for our input to church-planting and leadership training. Under prophetic encouragement we are seeking to take this seriously.

In 1997 we held our first International Summer School.

Its thirty participants were mainly people who were looking to learn about and experience church-planting into youth culture with a view to reproducing a similar dynamic in their own context. Furthermore we have had a number of 'open weekends' when anything from thirty to fifty leaders from a wide variety of backgrounds have come for a condensed exposure to the values expounded by the summer school. In the future we are planning to hold a weekend of this type in partnership with the Sublime Youth Congregation (led by Billy Kennedy and part of the Community Church in Southampton), NGM (led by Ray and Nancy Goudie) and Soul Survivor (led by Mike Pilavachi). Different streams coming together, but with an identical purpose and goal.

Creativity

As we have shown, the Celtic Christians were discipled in a contemporary cultural context where art was more developed than anywhere else north of the Alps. They were familiar with, and often trained in, the arts and crafts of illumination, bardic performance and song. The *Book of Kells* is but one staggering example of how this art was applied to their Christian worship.

Since the Reformation, there has been a very negative view in the West of anything that might suggest icono-clasm of 'idolatry'. The material/spiritual dualism of the Enlightenment is reinforced in exalting reductionist thinking, forensic theology and public preaching over the potential ambiguity and potential shallowness of art and symbolism. Thus, as Evangelicals, we have been discipled in a tradition that apparently affirms an environment of sparseness rather than beauty; of barrenness rather than richness.

Into this context the charismatic meeting in the drab school hall, the liturgy of 1960s-based guitar folk/rock and the lack of symbolism easily becomes the norm. The Celts have challenged us to review this lack of creativity. We have begun to experiment with different musical styles. Being blessed with some musicians who can play in an Irish folk style enables us to explore those resonances of Celtic culture that remain in the contemporary fiddle/whistle genre. We have tried rearranging some familiar worship sounds in the style of the Stax label (*aka* Blues Brothers). We have also tried non-melodic percussion-based worship with total audience participation! On top of this there are different forums within the diversity of the church which will be expressing different cultural motifs. For some the decks, the DJ and the MC are where things are moving. For others reaching business culture, this is not the way forward!

Visually we are drawing on the gifts of artists in our midst. They are painting or modelling the message at the same time as it is being preached, sung or prophesied. When we obtain our own building it will free us to use a multitude of backdrops, as well as video, computer graphics and other communication media. We want the place to bear the hall-mark of a God-loving, life-affirming community!

In all of these scenarios our aim is to promote a constant interaction and fermentation involving prayer, the creative, the apostolic and the heart of God for justice and involvement in society.

Spirituality

We have dwelt at length on the subject of spirituality in earlier chapters. However, there are one or two challenges we want to draw out here.

We are particularly fascinated that the Celts lived in a day before the godless philosophy of rationalism brought us the separation of nature and super-nature. For them God's wisdom held all things together. He broke in to the usual order of things by his wisdom when he chose. He responded to faith and to prayer in a way that is often beyond our finite minds. Often we have to struggle against a mind-set of scientific rationalism. We find it so hard to believe. We can tell stories of signs and wonders, but we long for more. It is the same when it comes to praying into the unseen world.

We are grateful to those in our church who are pioneering intercessory prayer. We know that the prayer life of the Celtic church showed tremendous energy and commitment. These men and women were not simply going through set prayers. They were covering their communities, their lives, their families in prayer. We want to move forward in our prayer life; to have that gentle simplicity matched with passionate energy that our 'Abrahams' before us had.

The prayer aspect of our community continues to develop both at grass-roots and in the intercessory team which consists of around fifty people. One of our aims is to see a centre of prayer established which will pray for twenty-four hours a day. Who knows how this will be achieved?

Discipleship

The last example is discipleship. The 'soul friend' concept recurs through so many Celtic stories. The biographies provided in Appendix 1 show how so many of the great leaders of the Celtic church owed their walk with God to their predecessors.

Over the years we have encouraged and modelled a pattern of discipleship and accountability that has the same heart as the soul friend. We have aimed at transparency as leaders. To confess our sins to one another. To keep short accounts. To speak the truth in love to one another. The heart of our cell life, our training modules and our pastoral care have all been permeated strongly by these values.

The two of us have stood by one another in times of great celebration and also in times of darkness. We have prayed with one another and despaired at one another! Two men who are very different and yet who know a bonding as soul friends.

It is not good for a person to be alone. We thank God for our marriages and for our advisors. But, as somebody once said, a person without a soul friend is like a body without a head.

Summary: New Celts today

They were an indigenous people who first brought the gospel to a pagan British culture . . .

. . . *we face the same mission challenge today.*

They lived simply and positively with creation and depended on signs, symbols and supernatural manifestations of God . . .

. . . *all very appropriate to post-modern Westernism.*

They were wild and aggressive, as well as reflective and worshipful, in their spirituality . . .

. . . *sound familiar?*

Their music runs closest to the 'earth rhythms' of our geography and therefore its recovery is part of uncovering our 'new rhythm' . . .

. . . Celtic music seems to be striking a fresh chord with many people at the moment, including dance music.

'Celtic spirituality' has been ripped off and hijacked by New Agers who emphasise its pagan form . . .
. . . all the more reason to recover its orthodox Christian expressions.

The wellspring of Celtic Christian spiritual life in these islands has been blocked over the past millennium by two things: (a) the domination of a Roman 'control' model of church, leading to Christendom, dualism and the corruption of the authentic gospel; and (b) the political oppression of the Celtic tribes by the English tribes . . .
. . . as we enter the next millennium let us get hold of our roots, foster a reconciliation between the Celtic peoples (Welsh, Scots, Irish, Cornish and whoever else!) and the English peoples, re-evangelise these islands and become the New Celts today!

Bibliography

The titles below are those which will directly expand on some of the material we have covered in this book. For deeper study, we recommend the bibliography in Ian Bradley's *The Celtic Way* which is divided into subjects. There are also some excellent bibliographies available on the Internet.

Bede, *Ecclesiastical History of the English People* (Penguin).

Ian Bradley, *The Celtic Way* (London: Darton, Longman and Todd, 1993).

Ian Bradley, *Columba: Pilgrim & Penitent* (Glasgow: Wild Goose, 1996).

Peter Brandon, *The South Saxons* (Chichester, 1978).

E. H. Broadbent, *The Pilgrim Church* (London: HarperCollins, 1931).

F. F. Bruce, *The Spreading Flame* (Glasgow: Paternoster, 1958).

Thomas Cahill, *How the Irish Saved Civilisation* (New York: Anchor Books/Doubleday, 1996).

Nora Chadwick, *The Age of Saints in the Early Celtic Church* (Oxford: Penguin, 1961).

John Dawson, *Healing America's Wounds* (Regal).

Tim Dowley (ed.), *The History of Christianity (A Lion Handbook)* (Oxford: Lion, 1990).

N. Higham, *The English Conquest I: Gildas and Britain in the Fifth Century* (Manchester University Press, 1994).

David Marshall, *The Celtic Connection* (Grantham, 1994).

John Marsden, *The Illustrated Life of Columba* (Floris Books, 1995).

Henry Mayr-Harting, *The Coming of Christianity to Anglo-Saxon England* (London: B.T. Batsford, 1972).

Michael Mitton, *Restoring the Woven Cord* (London: Darton, Longman and Todd, 1995).

Gerald Murphy (ed.), *Early Irish Lyrics* (Oxford: Clarendon Press, 1956).

Stuart Murray, *A Loser's Guide to Church History* (Chichester, Pioneer Equipped to Lead, Revelation Centre, PO Box 58, Chichester PO19 2UD, 1997).

Stephen Neill, *A History of Christian Missions* (London: Penguin, 1986).

T. G. E. Powell, *The Celts* (London: Thames and Hudson, 1990).

M. Winterbottom (ed.), *Gildas. The Ruin of Britain and Other Works* (Chichester: Phillimore, 1978).